Once Upon an Expat

AN ANTHOLOGY

EDITED BY

Lisa Webb

CANADIAN EXPAT MOM

Once Upon an Expat: An Anthology

First edition copyright ©2016 Lisa Webb

ISBN-10: 6027333529
ISBN-13: 978-602-73335-2-9

Copyright ©2016 Lisa Webb

Interior Design by editordeluxe.com
Cover design by Emir Orucevic

Published by Canadian Expat Mom

A Note from the Editor

When I first had the idea for this book, getting started was slightly intimidating. I didn't know what kind of response I would get—if any at all. But I knew that as an expat I had stories to share, and if I did, others must too.

What came flooding into my inbox were tales so rich and bold that my initial insecurities were but a fleeting memory.

I am beyond proud to introduce you to this group of strong, global women, who through their words, have made me feel like I have found my tribe. They pour out their experiences of life abroad to make up the pages of *Once Upon An Expat*.

All author royalties for this book are being donated to help promote children's literacy and education in developing countries.

Staying true to the authors' countries of origin, in these stories you will find spelling conventions vary with 'neighbor' and 'neighbour', 'traveled' and 'travelled', along with punctuation from the US, UK, Canada, and Australia.

To all those that have been brave enough to embrace the ups and downs of living in a foreign country. May the fond memories outweigh the hardships.

And to my expat friends who get me through this wild ride with my sanity intact.

Table of Contents

Europe 1

My (Naked) French Manicure *Lisa Webb*........................3

Pride and (Bus) Prejudice *Jasmine Mah* 7

Transition Woes in Ukraine *Leah Evans*......................11

Losing My Grandmothers *Amanda van Mulligen*..........18

Le Bonjour *Carole Clark*..23

Riding the Subway *Amélie Sánchez*..............................28

Silent Competitions and Busted-up Bus Stop
Conversations *Nitsa Olivadoti* 35

Baby Bumping in France *Ashly Jeandel* 40

One Trip Guaranteed to Stretch Your Marriage
Kathryn Streeter 46

Sun Worshipers *Olga Mecking*......................................54

A Paris Job Ain't All Macarons *Lizzie Harwood*...........58

Africa..**63**

Diary of a Mom in Congo *Cecile Dash* 65

Lost in Libya *Lesley-Anne Price* 76

An Unbelievable Bus Ride *Camille Armantrout* 83

Mrs. Matt in West Africa *Sarah Murdock* 91

Middle East **103**

Forbidden Falconing *Chandi Wyant*...........................105

The Price of Beauty *Margaret Ozemet* 112

Returning Home *Michelle Estekantchi* 122

The Land of No Logic *Margo Catts*.............................128

Asia...**137**

A Man from Another Land *Shannon Day* 139

Coming of Age in the Middle Kingdom
Carissa Cosgrove..143

Stranded on a Non-Deserted Island *Lisa Webb*...........153

A Celebration of Problems and Resolutions – A Very
Expat Christmas *Ersatz Expat* 163

Colours That Do Not Exist *Marcey Heschel* 172

A Year of Magic, Mystery and Chaos *Gabrielle Yetter* . 179

The Dawn *Kimberly Tremblay*...................................... 183
Feels Like Home *Nicole Webb* 187
Australia... **195**
Here's a Tip on the Tip *Kristine Laco* 197
North America **201**
Are You an Expat If You Don't Know You Are?
Robin Renée Blanc... 203
Wasting Away in Paradise *Stephanie De La Garza* 209
Confessions of an Expat *Tina Celentano*..................... 213
South America.. **217**
The Making of a Brazilian Body *Brynn Barineau* 219
What Mattered Most *Sally Rose* 226
No Fixed Address **231**
How Not to Say Goodbye *Catriona Turner*................. 233
Yes, Me Too! *Rosemary Gillan*.................................... 241
The Evolving Vocabulary of the Expatriate Life
Akajiulonna Patricia Ndefo... 248
The Ripple Effect *Angie Benoit*.................................. 251
When Going 'Home' Isn't a Clear Choice
Jennifer Hart 256
Choices *Janneke Muyselaar-Jellema* 261
Lost and Found Between Homeless and Homeful
Amel Derragui 271
Acknowledgements... 274
About the Contributors... 275
About Canadian Expat Mom 291

Europe

My (Naked) French Manicure
Lisa Webb

When you quit your job and move to a country where, upon arrival you don't speak the language, it can be tricky to figure out just what to do with yourself during the day.

I chose to make babies. They're cute and cuddly; they smell good and generally make you smile. From what I'm seeing around me, I can only assume there are other expat moms who have had the same idea.

As much as we love these babies, there comes a time when we need a break, and want to be away from them, even if for just a few hours. This can be tough to manage when your family lives on the other side of the world and your local friends are in the same situation. Why would they want to take my baby, when they're looking for a little break from their own rug rats?

In come the husbands. They stepped up to the plate to do some solo parenting while the wives had a morning at the spa, one fine January day in the south of France.

I was pregnant at the time, and there was no pregnancy

massage table, so a massage for me was not an option. I could have opted for the mud wrap, but when you're pregnant, and feeling big already, there's nothing appealing about being rolled in mud. So I decided to get a manicure. If I were huge, at least I'd have nice nails.

Since there was a fairly big group of us that morning, we had the entire spa to ourselves. We felt like the 'Real Housewives of Small-town Southern France', even if it was just for that morning; we'd take it. We spent the next few hours bouncing between the Jacuzzi, hammam, sauna, sitting in our spa robes nibbling croissants and taking turns going in for treatments.

When it came time for my manicure, I was ready to be pampered, dressed for the part in my crisp white spa robe and matching slippers.

I follow the aesthetician into the treatment area, where we pass my friend Mary already set up at a manicure station, also getting her nails done. As I pass Mary, I flash a quick smile and a wink in her direction, wondering how she's making out with her French small talk.

The woman brings me past my friend, and the manicure station, down a hallway, and into a dimly lit room with a massage table. Clearly there's been a mistake.

"*Je suis ici pour mes ongles,*" (I'm here for my nails) I tell her. She confirms that she knows and hands me the disposable, see-through panties that they give you for massages, telling me to take off my bathing suit and put those on.

Has my French really gotten that bad? She must not have understood me? I repeat myself, "*Je suis ici pour mes ongles. Pour une manicure.*" She again confirms that she knows, tells me to put on the little panties and that she'd be right back.

Left alone in the room, I'm not sure what to do. If I'm here for my nails, why do I need to get undressed? After all, I just walked by Mary, fully clothed, and getting a perfectly normal manicure. But the thing about living in a foreign country and not being completely confident with the language, is that sometimes it's just easier to 'go with it' instead of asking questions.

So off comes my bathing suit, and on go the tiny disposable panties. *Which way is the front? Is it a thong? A double thong?* This is always an issue and a great story for another time. But for right now, I'm too confused to care, and just throw them on, and quickly put my robe back on because why would I stand there naked to get my nails done. Right?

A moment later she's back and instructs me to take off my robe. Okay, this time it's got to be my French? Why does she want me to get naked? I try one more time, "*Je suis ici pour mes ongles.*"

She's starting to get irritated with me, or maybe thinks I am a slow learner. With a sigh, she tells me that she knows and instructs me again, to take off my robe and give it to her. Not wanting to irritate her further, I pass her my robe and stand facing her, totally confused, slightly embarrassed, and wearing nothing but the tiny see-through panties she gave me. I start to think that I might be on a hidden camera show.

I'm instructed to climb up on the massage table, and as I lie on my back, completely exposed, my eyes are searching the room for the hidden camera. But this is the nicest spa in town; there's no camera. I'm just in southern France, where nudity, apparently, isn't really that big of a deal.

Eventually she covers me with a towel and does my entire manicure with me lying on the massage table.

When I make my way back to my friends they greet me with, "So, how was your manicure?"

"Naked." I say with a deadpan face. "I was completely naked."

Reading their faces was a quintessentially expat moment for me. I know you can't judge an entire country on one person alone, but in this case, that's exactly what I did.

The expressions on the faces of the friends before me spoke volumes of the countries they came from. I had looks of shock, and giant question marks across the faces of those that represented Canada, Scotland, Australia and the US. But then I glanced over at my French friend, and in perfect representation of her country, she simultaneously raises her eyebrows, shrugs her shoulders and lets out a blasé 'pfff' sound, as if I just told her something as boring as 'I had eggs for breakfast'.

I still don't know why I was given a naked manicure that day and I probably never will. Maybe she didn't want me to have to stay in a wet bathing suit? Maybe she didn't feel like waiting for Mary's manicure to be done?

Whatever the case; this is life in a foreign country where you're learning the language. You can find yourself in strange situations that would never happen at home. Sometimes you're able to pull together the vocabulary and actually ask the questions you need to, and other times, you can't be bothered; and you find yourself standing naked in a dark room with a strange woman, when all you wanted was to get your nails done.

Vive la France!

Pride and (Bus) Prejudice
Jasmine Mah

My journey to living in Italy starts out as all good stories do—with an Italian boy in tight white pants. I was a meagre nineteen years old when we met almost eight years ago in Alberta, Canada, a moment in time that coincidentally coincided with the moment I fell in love with Italy. Funny how that happens isn't it?

I always considered myself exponentially more prepared than your average American expat in Italy, and I certainly never bought into that "I'll learn Italian by osmosis when I get there" concept they've been trying to sell us via the perfect vessel of Diane Lane in *Under The Tuscan Sun*. No sir, I applied myself and took Italian in university alongside a wonderfully light course load called my undergraduate pharmacy degree. I religiously recorded every episode of *House Hunters International* that featured a strong female lead moving to Italy (forcing my parents to watch it as evidentiary proof that I wasn't crazy and that other young women moved there all the time), and finally, I likely owned every travel literature book ever written on the subject. I was literally on my second copy of Marlena De

Blasi's *A Thousand Days in Venice* because I wanted that to be my life. I had done the dress rehearsal several times, and when I finally moved to Italy last year, it was not my first rodeo by any means. I was *prontissima* (the suffix emphasizes the word 'ready', equivalent to 'super, duper ready'). There would be no fooling me, no behind-the-back snickering as I unknowingly ordered a cappuccino after midday to accompany my Margherita pizza; I was well-versed in the cultural no-nos. Turns out, the most cringe-worthy expat moments tend to come when you least expect them, no matter how prepared you are. Mine came while I was waiting for the bus.

Now I know how to take a bus, in fact, I have stellar bus-taking capabilities and on this particular day, just a few after my arrival in Italy, I had already expertly surpassed the initial foreigner mistake of not knowing that you have to buy your ticket before boarding the bus. Ha! So there I was, ticket in hand like a real Italian, waiting at the bus stop and smiling like a fool at my ingenuity. *Eccolo* (there it is)! My bus is rolling up. Imagine it in slow motion like Richard Gere in a limousine, minus the flowers. I started walking towards it and zoom…it whips right past me! I am perplexed. Baffled even. In Canada, buses stop at bus stops.

My mind started making up rational excuses to explain what just happened: I was too short, the driver was colourblind, I was at a fake bus stop, this was one of those comedy shows where they film your reaction to a laugh track, and of course, I thought perhaps it was a race issue or prejudice against overly-tanned racially-ambiguous Canadian girls.

It was noon and the next bus would pass in another hour and a half. Fine, I reasoned with myself. I'll pop into the grocery store across the street and peruse. Seventy minutes and two bagfuls of perusing later, I teeter-tottered back to the same stop. I "teeter-tottered" because I was dutifully wearing heels like a good wannabe-Italian should.

Right on schedule (surprisingly), another bus sped right on by, leaving me, literally, in the dust with a gaping mouth. You're probably wondering why, at this low point, I didn't break out my "so-called" expert Italian skills and ask for help. Instead, there I was, sincerely concerned about being stranded overnight instead of getting the information on the bus system. It's the fault of the greatest expat demise, the P word: pride. How could I live with myself and my self-actualized blog if I couldn't even figure out how to take the bus in my adopted country? I mean, it's a bus, not a Rubik's cube and even if it were one, I heard Justin Bieber can solve it in two minutes. I was a failure of an expat, unable to accomplish the simplest task of getting on a bus.

Well, *amici*, I spent the greater part of that day at that bus stop. I hate to admit it, but I had already worked out how many days my groceries would sustain me and was eyeing a cardboard box as shelter when a young Italian boy sauntered over. Like clockwork, a bus came around the corner and the boy stuck out his arm as if hailing a taxi and...THE BUS STOPPED.

If there were ever an opportune time to say "eureka" it would have been this. I, on the other hand, used a different word. I could've hugged that boy. In fact, I might have. His arrival was akin to the second coming of Jesus for me that day. Anyway, the moral of the story is buy a car to drive in Italy and never take public transportation. Just kidding, that's what I told my Italian-in-white-pants to convince him to chauffeur me around the city on-demand my first weeks in Italy.

The real lesson is that as an expat, you have to forget about pride. Never be too ashamed to ask for help along the metaphorical or literal journey that is the adventure of living abroad. Oh, and remember that you have to hail buses in Italy.

Transition Woes in Ukraine
Leah Evans

With every new country, I get worse at acclimating. No matter how excited I am about the country or how ready I am for the move, I still go into serious culture shock upon arrival. Some people take less than a month to adjust, some take two or three, but I now need the full six months before I enjoy where I am, understand the culture, and love my life. This is a story of acclimation and culture shock. It isn't a critique of Ukraine, where I had recently moved, or the United States, my home country, or Ecuador, the country where I was previously posted. It is just about how we are hit with the unexpected and how some handle it gracefully and some do not. I've never been known for my grace.

I arrived in Kyiv, Ukraine on an unusually hot June day, and the heat wave continued for the next few weeks. I was five months pregnant and utterly miserable. I felt huge, sluggish, and foggy. My girls were one-and-a-half, three, and five years old. They were sweet and helpful, at times, but they also struggled with the move. We went into our temporary apartment on the fourth floor of a quaint old building. The beautiful windows swept to the high ceilings, flooding the rooms with light, and heat. Unfortunately, the windows did not have locks. With three little girls I was terrified the entire time we lived there that one of my acrobatic children would climb up on the windowsills and fall out. But I did like the apartment because it was big, spacious, and in a great location. I didn't like the fact that the electricity went out constantly, usually right when I was trying to go out. One time in particular, instead of calmly taking the elevator, I wound down four flights of stairs in the center shaft of the building in complete darkness. I had to carry my double stroller and my one-and-a-half year old, while pregnant, in the heat and darkness. By the time I got to the bottom of the steps, I was sweaty, frustrated, and anxious. I did it though because my kids wanted to go to the park and we had waited for hours, but the electricity just wouldn't come back on!

We walked down the hill to a lovely little park with a kids' jungle gym. My kids were jet-lagged and unhappy with the move. As I walked up to the park, I saw that it was full of lovely women with casual and beautiful hair, classy clothes, and shoes I wanted to steal. For, not only was I five months pregnant, I was also wearing Wal-Mart maternity clothes. For those of you who don't know, Wal-Mart is as far from stylish and classy as you can get. Pregnant for the last time, I didn't want to spend too much money on clothes for my expanding body. At that moment, I seriously regretted the decision. On top of it all, I wore tennis shoes. In most countries, wearing tennis shoes is the same as tattooing a sign on your forehead that says, "I'm an American tourist." I didn't usually wear tennis shoes but our first night in Ukraine we had gone for a long walk. An extremely drunk man had lurched by us and fell on top of me, stepping on my brand-new sandal and tearing the strap right off. I was fine, although overwhelmed by his smell and horrified that my only non-sneaker footwear was now not functional. I immediately limped back to the apartment and changed shoes (and clothes).

Back to the park. It was beautiful, green, and lush. There was a playground surrounded by green lawn and shaded by tall trees. The weather was hot, but the warm breeze felt delicious. I told the girls to go and play so I could sit by myself and recuperate. It had been a tough morning. But, they didn't. My eldest stayed next to me asking over and over again when I was going to find her some friends. My second, totally out of character, was spitting at me. Over and over. My third launched herself at me because she wanted me to hold her but my back hurt so much from holding her all the time that I was ignoring her.

So, I did the only thing I could do—I started to cry beneath my sunglasses. We maintained our positions for some time and then I heard a kind voice say my name. I turned and realized it was my husband's boss' wife!

We had met the day before when she had kindly taken us to a party and introduced us to a bunch of welcoming and interesting people (many of whom would later become dear friends). I tried to pretend that I wasn't actually crying behind my sunglasses and we had a quick conversation as she made several recommendations for ice cream places we might want to visit. She very kindly didn't mention my smudged mascara. And then, thankfully, she left.

I started to cry again.

Not long after, my phone rang. It was my husband.

He said, "You know, the strangest thing just happened. My boss just came in and suggested that I go home and be with my family. He said that moving is always really hard, especially with little kids, and I should go home and have dinner with you guys."

I cried harder with happiness. He came home, we had a lovely dinner, and things were much better the next day.

But, they weren't perfect, of course. I was pregnant after all, and that meant I had to go to the doctor for a check-up. I was nervous about that because I had visited a doctor in a previous post in Tbilisi, Georgia, where I was accused of having chlamydia. Chlamydia is a sexually transmitted disease that can damage your fallopian tubes and make you infertile. I had a one year old at the time and went to the doctor to discuss having a second. He welcomed me into his office, furnished with a ripped old leather couch, an empty desk, and a chair. I told him I wanted advice about getting pregnant again and he told me I probably couldn't, because of the chlamydia.

"What chlamydia? How can you diagnose me with chlamydia without a test or an exam?"

"Well, you probably have chlamydia because you are American. You get it from sitting on concrete benches in the winter like all of you Americans do."

"I thought chlamydia was a sexually transmitted disease?"

"No, it comes from sitting on cold benches in the winter and it scars your fallopian tubes and then you can't get pregnant."

"Well, it can't be that bad because I think America has a pretty high birthrate."

But, this would be different. I walked into the nicest clinic in Kyiv and was warmly welcomed into an examination room by a doctor and two nurses. They told me to undress and get into the chair. I looked at them like they were crazy.

Now? Here?

They nodded and just kept watching me. So, I took off all of my clothes and heaved my heavy body into a chair that looked like what you would get into at the dentist but with most of the seat missing. Then, just like at the dentist, they cranked me up to eye level.

"Are you going to close the curtains?" I asked, as I gazed out at a lovely park with a winding walking path.

"No, there usually isn't anyone out there," the doctor said as he proceeded to examine me. I decided to screw my eyes shut and think about the extreme lengths doctors in the US take to ensure privacy and modesty. I tried not to think about what I looked like perched up high in the dentist/birthing chair. I tried not to have the baby right then and there.

Please know that I'm not insulting the way doctors do things in Ukraine. When I went back to the US months later to have the baby, I was annoyed with how the doctor or nurse would bring you into the room and then leave for you to get undressed. I wanted to say, "Just stay, I can get undressed in one second and then you can do your examination and we can all get out of here half an hour earlier!" There is nothing worse than sitting in a cold waiting room wrapped in a paper sheet while the doctor sees six other patients before they remember that you are there. There is something efficient about a lack of modesty.

But, at that moment in Ukraine, I was horrified, and embarrassed, and felt my Puritan American roots very keenly. I had never felt so exposed and unattractive in my life, but the nurses and doctors were professionals and quickly and efficiently did their work and lowered the chair. Then, they watched me get dressed, discussed my pregnancy, pronounced me healthy, and released me. The entire trip took about twenty minutes.

As a celebration, I took my children to McDonald's for ice cream cones. I figured I had the best chance to figure out the menu there. I strode up to the counter, asked my kids what flavor they wanted, and turned to the cashier. Using my small collection of Russian words, I ordered one vanilla and two chocolate cones to go. The man just stared at me. I tried again, using different words. He continued to stare. So I went for the desperation move and acted it out. I held up three fingers, then pantomimed eating an ice cream cone. I pointed two fingers at the brown counter and one at his white shirt.

Deadpan, he looked at me and said in perfect English, "So, are you saying you want ice cream cones?"

"Why didn't you start with that," I snapped, "since you heard me speaking English when I came in?"

"I just wasn't sure what you were doing," he said.

I swallowed hard, smiled, and reminded myself to be kind. Not only to the poor clerk at the counter, but also to myself. I was clearly sensitive about my language skills but at least I was trying. He wasn't mocking my attempts to speak Russian; he was actually trying to figure out what I was trying to say. Unsuccessfully, of course. So, I smiled, thanked him (in English), gathered the ice cream cones and fled for one of the lovely green parks found on almost every corner.

From there, of course, it just got better. I reminded myself daily about being kind to myself and to those trying to welcome me. My Russian ordering skills got better. My modesty disappeared. I met lovely people and visited amazing sights. I fell in love with Kyiv, just as most do. I had my son and returned to the beautiful white winter scene that is Kyiv in December. I took almost daily photographs of the blue and gold spires of St. Sophia and

St. Michael's cathedrals while out on my freezing morning runs. I never went back to McDonald's because there were so many other delicious cafés and restaurants to sample. I ate more than my share of cinnamon rolls, hot chocolate, *borscht*, and *vareniki*. I came to love Kyiv and forgot all about how hard it was to break in and feel at home.

When it came time to leave I cried, just as when I came in. And then, I went through it all again at the next post, only with different stories. And a little more kindness straight from the beginning.

Losing My Grandmothers
Amanda van Mulligen

I once read that it's easier to distance yourself from the death of loved ones when you are an expat. The loss doesn't seep into every cranny of your daily life. If you can't attend the funeral it's possible to picture your loved one at home getting on with daily life; it's easy to pretend death hasn't knocked. It's not a premise I relate to. My expat life hasn't felt like a shield during those times when death has swooped upon my family.

I had been a mother for ten days when I had my first experience of death as an expat. I'd barely physically recovered from the traumatic labor and birth both my newborn son and I had experienced when I got the call from my mother, telling me simply and sadly, "She's gone."

It wasn't news out of the blue. My precious grandmother had suffered a stroke months before. I'd made the crossing from the Netherlands to England in a highly pregnant state to visit her in the Royal Berkshire Hospital, coincidentally the same hospital I had made my entry into the world in.

As I entered the ward with my husband, mother and

aunt, and headed for my gran's bedside, there was a hopeful flicker of recognition in her eyes. Her lips turned up; she was trying to smile but the stroke had paralyzed the left side of her face and her right side had been significantly weakened. I took off my coat and put my bag under the cold metal hospital chair that sat expectantly by her bed. Sterile smells invaded my nose. I reached for my gran, I held her in my arms; she felt unfamiliarly fragile and vulnerable.

I sat and reflected on how much thinner her face had become since I saw her at her eightieth birthday celebration a few months back. Happier days filled with family and laughter. I noted how much dimmer the light in her eyes had become in the months that had passed.

My gran loved to talk, to chat, to tell stories. Silence usually had no chance with my gran, but the stroke had robbed her of that joy. There were noises, there were attempts to write down words for us and there were endeavors to share smiles and laughs but there was no escaping the fact that her voice had been stolen from her. We shared special moments around her sick bed, but the essence of my grandmother had been taken away by the stroke. Who she was had become locked up inside her own body.

When the time came to leave her I could hear pieces of my heart splintering away. Would there be a next time? Would my unborn son ever get to meet her? No one knew which way this would go. She may recover; the hospital staff was working hard with her, but we knew that being trapped in her body, unable to freely communicate was my gran's idea of a living hell. Her will was not abundant. I soaked her up, the memories of her, the woman she was and the grandmother she would always be.

And so that call came. "She is gone." I had days to make arrangements to attend her funeral, but I had a ten-day-old baby. I was already emotionally raw before the bad news from my mother, and I was sleep deprived. I was breastfeeding and my son had no passport. I couldn't get the scenario straight in my head where flying to England with a couple of days' notice would work. I didn't go. Guilt engulfed me.

No matter how difficult a decision it was then, I have slowly, in the years since, found my own peace with the decision I had to make. It felt to me like I had said my good-byes in the hospital; expat life had forced that upon me. I felt that she would understand. I have never been able to completely come to peace with the fact that I was not there for my mother, standing at her side when she most needed me, and I'm not sure my mother has either.

All of that raced through my mind years later when my dad called to tell me that his mother, my remaining grandmother, was facing the end of her life.

That was no bolt out of the blue either. My grandmother had been diagnosed with cancer more than a year previously. In fact, it had seemed so long ago when the word cancer was first uttered and she had battled so hard and lived so bravely meanwhile, that it felt like she would just live forever in spite of it. It felt like she had ignored cancer and got on with her life. And then suddenly things changed and the cancer started winning.

She could have hours, days, or weeks. Nobody could say how long she had left, but her home nurse had declared that the end was in sight. I battled internally for days, struggling with my instinct to jump on a plane, not knowing whether to go against her wishes and take a seat by her deathbed. Would I be on time? Would she even know I was there? My dad had told me that she was in a peaceful sleep most of the time, with lucid moments few and far between.

Did I want my last memory of her to be the image of her lost battle against cancer? Or the last time I had seen her, laughing and chatting, nonchalant about this evil invader in her body, surrounded by loved ones at a family meal?

I have three young sons; the logistics of taking off last minute to England are complicated. My husband and I don't have a line of people who can look after my children at the drop of a hat. I couldn't rush to England to sit by my gran's side, only to do it again a week later to attend her funeral. Reality. Cold hard facts. Logistics. Heartache. Instinct. It was all thrown in a melting pot and stirred around and around until I no longer knew what to do for the best. I decided to wait for the weekend; it was a matter of a few days.

On the Friday night I checked out flights. I would speak to my dad in the morning and see how my gran was at that point, and then make a final decision about whether to travel that day.

At 5 a.m. a deafening shrill noise wrenched me from my dreams. It took a few seconds to register this unfamiliar sound so early in the morning. It was the telephone. My husband passed me the receiver.

"It's your dad," he whispered.

"Hello?"

"It's Dad. Your gran has passed away. She went peacefully in her sleep in grandad's arms a couple of hours ago," he relayed in a sad, factual, bewildered manner.

At that moment, miles away and overseas, I was completely and utterly alone in my grief. My loss was invisible to those around me. My regrets remained

21

unspoken. It was travel arrangements for a funeral I needed to make. No question this time around that I wouldn't be there. This time there was a coffin; there was a chance to stand supported by loved ones in the midst of my family's grief.

When I moved away from my home country, set new roots down in a foreign land and made a new life, I took physical distance from those I had grown up with, those loved ones who had played a starring role in my childhood. My grandmothers were just such people.

Throughout my life I have never lived around the corner from my grandparents for any great periods of time, but when I moved abroad fifteen years ago I put physical and emotional distance between them and me. It's not just the miles between; it's logistics. I have three children and a life abroad—it's never a question of just popping back over the North Sea to return to England.

Since moving overseas, my pot of memories has filled more slowly with moments spent with my grandmothers. They consist of milestone birthday and wedding anniversary celebrations. The majority of the memories I have of time spent with my grandmothers are from my childhood and they are happy affectionate recollections. Those are the memories that I want to hold onto and keep close, those are the stories I will pass on to my sons, not the cold reality of a missed funeral, travel arrangements made in haste, and grief that I can't quite find a place for because of the miles in-between.

Le Bonjour
Carole Clark

I grew up in Canada speaking both English and French and consider myself perfectly bilingual. Well, close to perfectly bilingual anyways. So when my husband, two daughters and I moved to Paris, France, as expats the language barrier was no concern of mine. I just got down to the business of settling us into life as usual abroad. Sure I didn't understand *everything* but I was able to flow right into all the standard banter necessary to get things done.

As time passed, I had to face the fact that my level of perfectly bilingual had its own set of issues. One may think that moving to the "City of Lights" is all la-dee-da and romantic all of the time, but actually it's a pretty steep cultural transition from the plains of Canada. I had travelled through Paris before, and was aware of the Parisian's reputation for being a little... um... rude. But, living it in your day-to-day turned out to be something quite different. As my purely Anglophone expat friends praised my Francophone abilities, I often replied that sounding like a foreigner had its benefits.

Where I really got stuck was my accent. You see I was

born in a French-speaking family, so even though I grew up speaking English and making it my primary language, my accent in French is virtually unnoticeable. That would seem like a good thing on the outset, but in reality got me more than a few dirty looks. Parisians are steeped in cultural rituals, and missing your mark on any of them automatically places you in the category of imbeciles. It's one thing if you slip up with a twangy American accent, but when you do it speaking French like the French, they just can't figure out what is wrong with you.

Let's take the bakery, for example. The bakery is a place where you go to buy bread, or other sublime baked goodies. It's simple, right? Wrong! Your bakery is the pillar of your community, providing the staging ground for a daily ritual that all your neighbours take part in. And the people behind the counter, well, they have the all-important job of deciding which perfectly crispy on the outside, and soft and chewy on the inside baguette you're going to go home with. Plus you see these people every day, sometimes twice, or even three times, so you kind of want them to be friendly and smiley when you arrive.

Herein lies one of my first French accent fails. You can't just walk in there and ask for your bread, as I so mistakenly did on many occasions earning me a tight-lipped reception and barely a sideways glance at the cash register.

What on earth was going on? When others walked in they immediately received an enthusiastic greeting and chipper chitchat as they perused the daily offerings. I watched in wonder as the vendor searched through the stack of baguettes looking for perfection, something she most certainly never did for me.

So I took it personally. What else could I do? I felt like the ugly duckling that could never fit in to this beautifully organized system. Is it because they know I'm a foreigner? I pondered with gloom. Did I tie my scarf wrong? Is this orange T-shirt just too loud for Paris?

Getting my daily bread became a task of foreboding, a moment of cultural alienation ending in a feeling that I was missing out on the crunchiest crusts and softest insides that baguettes had to offer. I clearly wasn't living the full French experience, and would have to settle for the second-class breads. That is until one day I realized the existence of the magical word, or rather, the magical pronunciation of the magical word that is "bonjour".

I'm not just talking about any "bonjour". A barely audible "bonjour" just slipped out there in a timid voice won't do the trick. No one's interested in a half-hearted "bonjour". I'm talking about a loud and triumphant "bonjour", one that really embodies *good-day*. You have to launch it out there like you mean it for the whole place to hear because you're saying it to everyone, and on top of that, you better be hitting those high notes as you're reaching the end of the word, which coincidently transforms into "Bon-jour-re!"

Once I became aware of this continuous shrill *chanson*, I wondered how I didn't notice it before. Every person walking through the door threw it out there creating a symphony of high-pitched chirps filling the space with cordial and convivial warm-fuzzies.

This realization was my ticket into the gang. After a few practice rounds in the privacy of my own home, I was ready to give it a try. The next time I stepped into the bakery, I gathered my courage and let'er rip. "Bon-jour-re!" I called out with a smile, and lo-and-behold my "bonjour" was met with a chorus of friendly falsetto "bonjours" from behind the counter. I was elated, and it didn't stop there.

When I asked for my baguette, the woman serving me asked how I would like it, "*Bien cuite? Ou pas trop cuite?*" (Crusty or lightly baked?) and then proceeded to rifle through the pile after I specified my preferences. My heart filled with joy as I received my trophy. This was not just any baguette, but one that was hand-selected and passed over with a friendly smile. As I counted out my euros I reveled in my small victory, I beamed at the cashier and she smiled back. As I tucked my baguette under my arm I ventured an "au revoir" using the same tones, which was met with a jovial "au revoir" in return.

I had arrived. No longer was I a rude French person not minding my manners, I was in the posse. I began using "bonjour" everywhere I went, as I picked up on its prevalence in most social situations, and in places that quite frankly as a Canadian it would have never occurred me to greet the room. For instance, at the doctor's office when you enter the very-quiet waiting room, in which case you should adjust your volume level, or when entering the pharmacy (another French institution that rivals the bakery and merits a story of its own).

Furthermore, it's expected that people in the room respond to whoever is greeting them. I relished the delicious feeling of being an insider as I responded in turn to the regally coiffed old ladies, stately gentlemen, impeccably dressed women and men who imparted a "bonjour" in my general direction.

It even worked one-on-one. When crossing paths with my neighbour in the elevator, or my custodian at the gate, a friendly and enthusiastic "bonjour" was enough to keep things pleasant and even improve our social interactions. The bus driver, the cashier, the postman... No one in France can resist the power of "bonjour".

As it turns out the lesson learned about *politesse* at the bakery spilled over into improving many aspects of my life in France, and by the way, the baguettes were worth the wait.

Riding the Subway
Amélie Sánchez

I check the time on my phone for the fifth time: it is 4:10. I have to wait another fifty minutes for Nicolas' afterschool club to be over, and then we will head home. Ahead of me, dogs of all sizes run around without leashes, their owners chatting happily by a large gnarly tree. As a couple of joggers pass by the bench I've elected for my anxious wait, I decide to walk around the gorgeous autumn landscape to ease the tightness of time around my neck. It is now 4:12; Alex must be looking at the blue pillars at the Münchner Freiheit station from the subway train. Funny name! It means Munich Freedom. I wonder if he is thinking about his own freedom.

I thought the time it took for our international assignment to become effective had provided plenty of time for our family to prepare for a new lifestyle abroad. We agreed to leave Connecticut, USA in November but our move didn't actually happen until ten months later. Of course, packing up the house, selling and giving away our belongings, and playing the wait-and-see game of selling home and cars was stressful, but there was enough adrenaline involved to keep us all going with a smile. The children, then nine and four, had time to have one more birthday party before we left, and finish the school year. It was perfect, in a way.

We were heading for Munich, Germany, for two years. There was a vague plan of returning to Connecticut afterward, but nothing was set in stone, especially with everything we owned packed in a small storage unit by the highway.

The ring of a bicycle bell startles me from my reverie and I jump to the side of the path just in time to let a mother pedal past me, with a trailer loaded with two kids and a basket of fresh produce in tow. I am still getting used to cyclists everywhere.

Time check: it is 4:24. I imagine Alex preparing to "alight the train" at Odeonsplatz—where four lines intersect and thousands of people rush across—weaving between human currents in the hope of catching the next subway before the doors slide shut. Will someone push my child while swiftly sliding between the closing doors?

Obviously, I have anticipated some difficulties with our move. The language barrier is the most prevalent of them all. We need to get groceries and public transportation tickets (have you seen the Munich underground system and its thousands of options for tickets?). Fortunately, Munich is home to many other expats (they compose almost 25 percent of the population!), so the English language is known and mastered by many of the people we need to talk to. Another hurdle is learning to live in an apartment building after years in a house. You only notice how noisy your family is when you begin to worry about the neighbors downstairs! I also expect all of us to miss home, most likely often at first, and feel prepared to provide comfort when needed. Finding doctors, dentists, and emergency rooms is far in the back of my mind, as well as adjusting to new stores and currency. We have become expats, this is going to be fun!

4:35, did he reach Lehel yet? That's the station surfers use when they don't bike to "the wave" on the Eisbach. It's amazing to watch them line up with their boards, waiting for their turn on the permanent artificial wave, and cheering each other on. Alex might have to move over to make room for someone's board. I smile at the oddity of a surfboard in the subway, and walk on toward the large hill in the middle of the park (we will find out in a few months that it is the best spot for sledding!). When I reach the top, slightly out of breath, I turn around and see the red roof of the school behind the trees.

Only a couple of weeks after the autumn term began at our international school, the physical education teacher reached out to me with a problem: my ten-year-old son will not change for sports with the rest of the class. Instead, he runs to the restroom and changes in a locked stall. At first, I think it is silly. Secretly, I am proud of my boy for sticking to what is important to him. In Connecticut, the only place he has known until our international move, this has never been an issue, because children are not typically expected to change as a group. In Europe though, things are different and the teacher is very worried about his self-esteem. I agree to talk to Alex about it.

"Why does it matter so much?" Alex asks at home later that day, "Why don't they leave me alone? My self-esteem is fine!"

After another couple of weeks though, the teacher is adamant: children will soon travel to a swimming pool and a sports hall, and they will have to stay as a group under the supervision of one teacher. Alex can't simply go off alone. And what if other children want to do the same thing? Having always given my son the privacy he asks for, it is the first time I have to handle such an issue. Sheepishly, I ask the teacher to handle it the best he can, and I will follow his lead.

That is not the only misery in Alex's life. In a world now made of all things new and novel, he feels restrained. He is suddenly in a school of lined desks and chairs, after his entire academic career was spent in a Montessori setting. He now has classes in French—weekly, and in German—daily, without wanting them. He was already unhappy about leaving the only home he'd had, he now has a daily reminder, at school: things are just not up to him.

And he has to change in front of his peers.

On the other side of the hill, a circular area surrounded by a stone wall overlooks the city. When the air is dry enough and clear of clouds, one can see the Alps in the far distance, dotted with snow on their pointy heads. Closer, the Frauenkirche and other churches stretch their steeples toward the sky, sketching the typical horizon of Munich. I sit on a bench next to a woman with her eyes closed. A squirrel with tufted ears jumps from tree to tree, scaring a few sparrows away. A couple of young men come and sit on the stone wall, each with a beer bottle in his hand. It is now 4:41 and my son has probably reached the Max-Weber-Platz station, where we always forget that the doors open on the other side of the train. He probably forgot today again.

Of course, Alex does enjoy most parts of his new life. Avidly keen on maps, he loves taking the subway. He memorized the maps quickly and reproduced the lines we take daily in his Minecraft world. He always asks to lead us through the meanders of public transportation, and does not make mistakes. He revels in his strong sense of orientation, as we simply follow him or confirm his choices after checking the map. He invents a game in which we have to guess the shortest way from one station to the next. Munich also teems with bakeries where he's allowed to go "shopping" on his own, sometimes, to then savor a fruit-covered pastry. On the playgrounds of the many parks in the city, children are encouraged to play without their adults. A big open grassy area, a water pump with a few gutters and removable dams attached, a climbing structure, a spinning device. Alex thrives there with his little brother, and trips to the park are a daily occurrence. He is even allowed to play alone in our building's courtyard. This newly found independence is marvelous. Alex can't get enough of it.

Very soon, he asked to return from school on his own. We are talking about a thirty-minute trip with a connection in the middle. Ten stations, that's ten opportunities for ill-thinking people to get on the train that my child rides. Ten places where anything could happen. Anything!

Munich is quite famous for its safety. It is common to see children as young as six years old cross the street on their own, a boxy backpack on their back, on their way home from school. On public transportation, it is rare to make any type of physical contact with strangers. People keep their distance, stay on the right side of the escalators, and avoid having to touch anyone. Any horsing around is typically accomplished by young teenagers who straighten up when you look at them slightly sternly. Yet when my own child explains that he is ready to take this trip on his own, I promise to think about it while shuddering inside. I then quickly come up with a list of Herculean (to me) tasks for him to complete: know our home address, learn all our phone numbers by heart (home and cells, Mom and Dad), and agree to call me as soon as he gets home. Oh, and no computer. When I run out of excuses, I *finally* allow him to go on his first trip.

At 4:47, at last, I name the feeling that has been nagging at me, just underneath the layer of worry. It is awe. I have felt this way before, of course, especially when Alex took his first steps many years ago! Just like he rejoiced to be finally faring on his own two feet, mouth wide open and laughter of disbelief in his belly, making step after wobbly step from the sofa to the coffee table, he now is faring with his own ticket and his own house key, zipping from station to station, from one side of town to the other. I am in awe! He is most likely getting off at Ostbahnhof now, our home station, filled with the smell of sausages and fresh bread all day. Ostbahnhof, the station with red walls, is another hub with many travelers rushing from one end of the day to the next, grabbing a cup of coffee or dragging a small suitcase on wheels behind them.

"Do you know that the color red accelerates the heartbeat? That's a scientific fact," Alex has noted before, while stepping on the escalator. I bet his heart beats fast now, at 4:49, as he is preparing to walk the last stretch home. Mine is beating quite fast too, and I walk quickly down the hill to be at school in time for Nicolas. In my hand, the phone I have not put away vibrates.

"Hi. I'm home."

In my head, I am singing, throwing confetti, dancing madly! He did it! We did it! Aloud, I simply reply, "Great! I'm getting Nicolas, and then we'll be home in about thirty minutes."

A few days later, the gym teacher catches me in the

corridor and announces that Alex has made huge progress. In one class that week, he agreed to change his socks with the group. In the following class the same week, he stayed with the group the entire changing time and has done so ever since. *Casually*. Only then do I realize that we had stripped him of any control over his life when we packed up and left. Without opportunities to make decisions that matter, he held on to *any* decision he could make. By finally riding the subway alone in our new world, Alex regained some of the commands of his own starship. Surely, this is a well-known and quite typical milestone in parenting, but it took expatriation for me to get there!

Silent Competitions and Busted-up Bus Stop Conversations

Nitsa Olivadoti

It was only months into our assignment in Germany when I found myself caught up in a daily frenzy. A simple trip to the supermarket had quickly become one of the most stressful activities. One day, I was feeling brave and decided to have a non-verbal fight with a man of vast impatience who had followed too close behind as I made my way to the register. He had been maneuvering ways to jump in front of me, huffing and puffing as he endlessly cleared his throat. If I only could speak German, I would turn around and perhaps advise him to get checked by his doctor. I was moving at a completely normal pace, perhaps even quicker than normal as I have grown accustomed to doing here. As he moved closer and I felt his breath on my neck, close enough to blow my hair around—I cringed.

I grabbed one item: a loaf of bread, which was sitting in

a basket at the end of the conveyor belt and was about to unload my things. Suddenly, I felt a gentle, firm nudging of his body against mine. I wanted to turn and yell at him, but my lack of language would reveal myself as an outsider. It would be revealed by my fair skin and blonde hair that I am not actually a local. Keep up the illusion, I reminded myself. Look like you fit in.

As I was about to put down my first item, he revved up to lunge and cut in line. Little did he know, I had been expecting this; I was prepared. He was not my first or last supermarket debacle.

There was that time when I had dropped a packet of blueberries, which scattered across the floor. Who decided to pack them in such flimsy containers anyway? I had come back from a trip home the previous day, where customer service was amazing. Jet-lagged and carting two overtired kids with me, my heart sank. I have learned that in Germany, if you drop something in the supermarket, you must clean it up yourself. I was even handed a paper towel when once a carton of cottage cheese exploded on the floor because I dropped it at the register. Again, I was with my children and I am pretty sure one of them tripped me or was complaining so much I had rushed. I began to smile because a tall man walked toward us. I was sure he was offering his help, but he used his height to step right over me. After the blueberries were stuffed back into their package, I felt too embarrassed to do anything else other than to purchase them. To my relief and amusement, one of my expat friends experienced the same story and bought the blueberries as well. The strange challenges and choices we have to make as an expat are unparalleled. Do we wash them vigorously or throw them away?

Anticipating the impatient man's next move, I casually

stuck my leg out and reached for a pack of chewing gum. This created a roadblock across the register aisle, which resulted in the loudest puff of breath yet. I almost giggled out loud as I gloated in my personal victory.

Maybe being alone abroad makes you strange; you find comfort in these trivial wins, to eventually find your place in a society that will never be yours.

I walked out of the store that cold, gray Munich morning with a skip in my step and a smirk on my face. I held my head high, never looking back. That day, I won the silent competition, the wordless fight.

But not all of our experiences with the general public or language are aggressive or competitive. Some days expat life is just plain funny. Later that week as we waited at the bus stop, an elderly woman struck up a conversation with our family. Although it is rare to be spoken to for the purpose of speaking, when it does happen I am always with my children and it is always with an elder. Usually it begins with either the comment my children are *so süß* (so sweet) or perhaps a negative comment that they are misbehaving (especially in the case where a millimeter of their foot is touching any sort of space which could possibly be sat upon). There are many words that I do not recognize when someone is angry although I can certainly get the gist of them.

As we waited for the tram on our way to the Fasching parade (Carnival) an older woman smiled and spoke to the children. I had painted their faces as per their request, as a pirate and a pirate kitty fighter, whatever that is, but that is another story.

She spoke so fast that my husband and I were only able to grasp pieces of what she said after the casual conversation about the weather, what the kids were dressed as, which train we were waiting for...

But after a few more sentences, it all got quite muddled together, as it often does for us. The thing about the German language is that many words are so long, that you sometimes cannot decipher whether you are hearing a full sentence or a single one-hundred-syllable word. On top of that, if you throw any Bavarian dialect into the mix, you have the perfect recipe for a linguistic nightmare.

"I think she was not all there because she said that her son lives in Budapest, fighting communism," my husband whispers to me. His German is light-years ahead of mine, although we are still both living in the Dark Ages. I burst out in laughter.

"No," I insisted, "she told us that she has a son who lives in Budapest and he has two children, ages four and six." I had the feeling that she was reflecting on her own grandchildren, whom she must be missing on this festive day. My interpretation made more logical sense. Anyhow, she didn't look crazy; she was a well-dressed, well-put-together, sweet old woman.

During these random interactions, it usually comes to a point when you can get so completely lost you begin to form two looks: one is pretending you understand and the second has pursed lips, neither smile nor frown. After all, you have no idea if she is telling you her son had just died tragically or whether her grandchild just took her first steps. You learn to remain stoic, yet not impolite, a true art form, taking this non-communicative yet appearing to be communicating stance.

You remain trapped, hoping they won't notice that you have slipped off the cliff and you are drowning in a ravine of misunderstanding. It is too late to ask if they speak

English; which would reveal a betrayal in letting them blabber on for so long. In order not to let them know you have wasted their precious breath, you glance casually at the minutes left until the tram pulls up and think to yourself, "Why in the world does it say zero minutes left to arrival and the tram is not sitting in front of me this very moment?"

This is the moment I realize that even though we do not speak German well, we have been Germanized to some extent. You finally let out a deep breath when you are able to part ways, pretending to be in a sudden hurry to rush onto the train with a simple "*Schönen Tag*" (good day).

"Are you sure about hearing the communist thing? I mean, it can't be," I ask my husband.

"Perhaps she is talking about social medicine, maybe her son is a doctor? He could be a politician? Let's look up some different spellings of the word communism in the German-English app," I say, hoping to find a similar word and solve the mystery with a few clicks of my phone.

But alas, I cannot find any words in German close to communism that were not the word communism itself. "You could write a piece about our busted-up bus stop conversations," my husband said.

"Yes, I think I should."

Deciding to live in a different country with different challenges is the bravest, strangest, hardest and funniest thing you could ever choose to do with your life.

Baby Bumping in France
Ashly Jeandel

I held the blue-and-white stick in my hand, the positive symbol staring back at me. After over a year of trying I was finally pregnant. I almost fell over with disbelief. I had been living in France for a few years with my French husband and we wanted this baby so badly. I was bursting with excitement. (I had used about twelve pregnancy tests in the last year whenever I thought there was a hint that I might have been pregnant.) I ran around our little French chalet with its weathered shutters thinking of how I was going to announce this to my husband.

To be honest, I was already thinking about how I was going to decorate the baby's nursery. It was truly a moment of pure happiness. After telling my husband, my thoughts jumped to the next person I would naturally tell, my Mom, but it was too early for me to call! That damn time difference. That's when I felt that feeling in the pit of my stomach; that moment when it really started to sink in that I wouldn't have my family around me at all for this experience.

I had always been the adventurer of the family. I know

that even though my mother was happy for me when I told her that my temporary nanny stint overseas turned into starting my own family in a small French village, she was cringing inside because of the distance that would be between us. My husband and I had planned this pregnancy, there were no surprises there, but I didn't expect the anxiety that shot through my body every morning when I woke up. Feelings of pure panic. A feeling of *what did I do???*

How could I, a first-time Mom, do this without my own Mom? Within minutes of this first panic attack I was on Amazon and ordered five books about being pregnant all written in English. I read through them and underlined everything I thought my husband should read (that he never did). What I didn't really realize at the time was that a lot of it pertained to the American baby-bump world. That was where my adventure began.

The pregnancy was confirmed by my general doctor and she gave us the name of an OBGYN, whose last name actually translated as "an orifice", which means any opening, mouth or hole in the body... enough said.

Not that I really gave my husband a choice, but he assured me he would be at every appointment to help translate. I'm a planner and the fact that I knew there was a lot coming my way made me nauseous, or maybe that was just the pregnancy. We walked into our OBGYN's spacious office. To my right was his desk decorated with sculptures of pregnant women and in the middle of the room a divider and to the left "the chair". After speaking to him for a few minutes he told me to go behind the divider and get undressed. So I did as I understood. Standing there I took off my shoes, then my sweater... wait. Did he say to get naked? No, it wasn't possible. I thought to myself, *where is my gown?*

In Canada you always disrobe and put on a hospital gown when seeing a doctor. I can't just be butt naked in front of him?

I quietly asked my husband in English if that is what I was supposed to do. He said he didn't know he had never been there before. I felt like strangling that oh-so-loving husband of mine. He always shrugs his shoulders when I'm having an expat moment. So he asked the doctor for me, I'm sure I was blushing, and the doctor said, *"Bien sûr!"* (of course). He was going to see me naked anyway, what should I be self-conscious about?

I kept telling myself to stop being such a conservative Canadian, and just get up on that chair. However he hadn't pulled off the paper from the previous patient so there I waited. Trying to cover my lady parts with my hands, feeling more out of place than I ever had in France. I wiggled my way over to the chair and with a deep breath, I sat down and closed my eyes.

Not that it mattered; he was the one doing the looking. I peeked to the left to see my husband standing there trying not to laugh; trying to be a grown-up. However just seeing him made me laugh, which made an already awkward situation even more awkward.

We conquered that first visit (until the next appointment where I felt equally uncomfortable), now there was just the whole 'being pregnant' thing to deal with. I never thought it would be easy, but I didn't expect what was to follow. I had the worst morning sickness, I was sick eight out of nine months.

We were in the process of building a house at the time so I spent most my time alone on the couch, not able to move or I would be sick. I always seemed to crave the things I couldn't have. I had dreams of my favourite

Canadian snack, Hawkins Cheezies, and just when my Mom would have them in the mail and they arrived, it would be another thing I couldn't eat.

I think no matter how old we get, if we built a strong bond with our parents when we were young, we still have this need to be close our entire lives. This space that seems only they can fill. That's how I felt on a normal day. I missed my Mom terribly. I was homesick for the small things that I had never even known were important. Now with all those pregnancy hormones flowing through my body, that feeling was amplified by ten. I would cry at the sight of a maple leaf. I would curse at my husband that it was his fault we were here. Then cry if he even suggested moving back to Canada. I was so confused, happy, afraid, lonely, homesick and excited. Sometimes all of these emotions were happening at once.

My husband was really advancing on our house project. It was growing up from the ground and my belly was also growing. It came time to find out if we were having a girl or boy. Like I said, I love to be prepared, so when my doctor asked if we wanted to know the sex of our baby, I replied with a quick, *"Oui"*. At least I knew the answer to that one in French. He then asked if I wanted my husband to know which confused me. I was sure I had misunderstood. However, he said that it is the mother's choice. I thought of how I could torture my husband over the next several months with all the teasing, but I snapped back to reality and I said yes he could know. The doctor announced, *"C'est une fille!"* I cried tears of happiness, and hormones were flying.

I don't know why it bothered me, but I guess when I dreamed of that moment, I just thought it would be in English. I love learning and speaking French but there was a part of me, my Anglophone Canadian side, that felt almost protective over these moments. It is still a feeling I have trouble describing today. It is like when we watched the new *Star Wars* movie in French, it is just not the same as the 'movie' I had imagined in my head. This feeling has often found its place in my life since having children, I have this urge to force English into those special moments. If only life had subtitles.

The big day finally arrived, four days of contractions was enough for me to not remember my native language, let alone a second language. I remember being unable to speak to anyone, I was so tired. They kept telling me it was too early, it was normal for this to happen. I was tired though, it was hard work. In France, a lot of the deliveries are done by midwives. They really are wonderful, except when they tell your husband he can go get lunch at a restaurant, it will be a while. I didn't want to seem like the bitchy wife who wouldn't let him go, so I shook my head repeating to him over and over in my head, hoping that the message would get to him telepathically, DO NOT LEAVE THE ROOM, I HAVE NO IDEA WHAT IS GOING ON.

Being in a foreign country, and having a baby in that country, means I didn't ask as many questions as I would have back home. I simply didn't know the words or maybe didn't know how to say it in the right way. I did though meet a lot of nurses. Everyone who hadn't spoken a word of English since high school was in my room, hoping to get in some free English conversation lessons… although I was less in the mood. After all that hard work and pain, I had to have an emergency C-section.

It was horrifying, my daughter was a big baby, and they had to pull like crazy, the table was swaying back and forth and still no baby. The doctors were talking but it just sounded like mumbles to me. After all those struggles, she was born. She was perfect.

I had an amazing weeklong stay at the hospital, where I was helped and showed the proper way to do things when we went home. I was nervous about this bringing my baby home, but like they say, it was natural. Though my husband might say I was a wreck for the first few months. And that's pretty much the end of my baby-bumping story...

Or so I thought. In France there is also this thing called perineal rehabilitation. Yes, I was nervous as soon as the midwife said it. I looked at my husband once again with this dumb confused look on my face, seeking some kind of help and he shrugged again. (If only I had had a baseball bat.) The idea of this rehabilitation is to work on your muscles 'down there'. There were a lot of different techniques and even an electrical 'tool'. I still blush just looking at it. I thought I was embarrassed before, jeez, this time I had to work with a midwife, and I had to imagine things like flowers and bridges, while tightening and releasing different muscles.

I really was perplexed when she told me to imagine raising a draw bridge; having me tighten when it got to the top and then drop it down quickly to release. It sounded to me like she wanted me to draw a picture or something. I thought I must have misunderstood. This couldn't be a muscle-tightening exercise? I mean, I get it. It is obviously important, but having a person who you don't know 'down there' tightening things will always be uncomfortable for me. But I live in France, *c'est la vie!*

One Trip Guaranteed to Stretch Your Marriage
Kathryn Streeter

If you consider your family life healthy don't test it by going to IKEA for the day, especially if you have recently moved overseas to an unfamiliar city such as London, with previous stops along the way in exotic-but-foreign places.

I've recently recovered from a family outing to a London IKEA after making just such a protracted international move. I'd prepared for our journey to IKEA well in advance, measuring every potential living and storage arrangement possible in our 900-square-foot flat. Except for clothing and personal effects we'd moved with nothing. Our flat was empty and a robust shopping trip was needed for items such as tomorrow morning's cup for my American cup-of-coffee.

London living is synonymous with flat living, spatial dimensions which mercilessly teased out the difference between wants and necessities. I spent several days combing IKEA's website and found exactly what we needed, down to trashcans and potato masher. In short, I meticulously filled over twenty notecards—front and back—with drawings, measurements, item numbers and color options.

This was no frivolous shopping trip: This was a new me on a new day and my husband wasn't remotely aware. My expectations matched the adrenalin that had overcome me to meet the challenge of the previous six months of constant motion and moving. The frenzy of the move commenced when my husband simply accepted a job in London. I sorted our earthly possessions, making three piles: save, give and sell. Especially tricky was separating out clothing suitable for the places and their corresponding climates we would be living in interim before heading to London where—if all went smoothly—we would reunite with our remaining clothing and some coveted personal items. We needed attire for several weeks in Scotland during July, a time of year that is more like fall in our home city of Washington, DC. From there we'd take up life indefinitely in Dubai, coinciding with their brutal summer temperatures. Lastly, we'd find ourselves thrust into gray, ever-wet London. Bone-chilling, rainy, short days explain London's winter.

The rest seemed easy in comparison: we packed all our earthly possessions and sent them to storage.

This entire experience had circled back and now I throbbed with an urge to nest. For me, this was an altogether alien yearning. When I was a new bride I had not felt this magnetic pull and neither had I felt this drumbeat after having babies. I had given birth to our firstborn in Germany, unable to participate in the conventional American baby shower tradition. Apparently our little newborn missed it even less than I did. For a few nights, she slept soundly in a suitcase. She had neither a legitimate nursery nor crib waiting her arrival, but I didn't regard that with disappointment as a first-time mom. No romantic dream had been shattered. Rather, seeing our daughter sleeping peacefully in a suitcase only increased the unmistakable miracle of birth amidst the brightness of that day's adventure. Up until now, I was the perfect wife for expeditions like this current whirlwind of a move.

But something quietly stored away inside me was preparing to blow. Internally, I held the impending IKEA visit and the transforming of our flat into a home with tight stomach and clenched fist. I wasn't going to lose.

However, there was much to negotiate. Going to IKEA wasn't just a long road trip like it was in Washington, DC. That would have been too easy. New to London and without a car like most, I'd carefully mapped out our train route. We would start early, hoofing it to catch London's renowned underground tube to the nearest central station. At the central station, we'd connect with an over-ground train that would take us to the outskirts of London where the behemoth IKEA could spatially fit.

Detailed study also presupposed assessing the nearest station to IKEA that offered a free shuttle service for customers. As transportation coordinator for this outing, I matched the train's arrival time and shuttle schedule so there would be minimal layover between our train arrival and shuttle pickup. We needed to maximize our Saturday and there was no room for error.

I had made the approximate time calculations required for the roundtrip, a flawless itinerary. But, indeed, it was going to be a long day. Every step needed planning especially since our grade-school aged children were along for the big day. That would most certainly involve frequent complaints of hunger pangs, bathroom breaks, dehydration gripes and other escape tactics.

Notecards in hand, I led the charge.

No more than forty-five minutes after our arrival at IKEA, my husband warily regarded my plump stack of notecards. His eyes pleaded, "Are we trying to do too much for one day?" Behind me, he was manning the large cart. Our daughter was holding his hand tightly and her little forehead was dimpled with worry. Dragging his feet, our son's body was draped over the cart. He begged for a break. "Aren't we done yet, mom?"

We'd not even made it through the monstrous living room showroom. "Guys, we've just begun!" I said cheerfully.

I heard a little voice: *Mayday. The team is going down.* I blithely ignored it.

We wove through the endless warehouse maze of showrooms displaying home furnishings and organizational solutions. I found myself dizzy with my notecards, commanding my halfhearted troops.

My husband's posture was thick with unease. His eyes spoke: "Where is the woman I married?"

Life had been as messy as it had been eventful. When we'd finally arrived in London, we lived temporarily in a furnished flat while searching for the perfect "home." It was not without a little triumph that I could now rattle off an address where I was physically, semi-permanently attached. *Home.* I felt entitled to this desire to banish all signs of unsettledness and all I was asking for was just one day at IKEA to help make that happen.

My arguments having failed, I couldn't at this point master my edgy body language. I defensively held my notecards, unmindful of the protests—some silent, others not—coming from the people dearest to me.

My husband's body language spoke back to me, a gentle but convincing questioning of my tactics. He understood the children's frustrations and they naturally looked to him for comfort. Blinded with focus, I was unmindful of their collective misery.

Our daughter's voice trembled, "My tummy hurts. I'm hungry, Mom." Our son yelped about needing to go to the bathroom again. Shoving a granola bar into my daughter's hand and clamping a hand on my son's shoulder, I restated my case. My husband's calm words of distress went unheeded.

After all, we were almost there. The battle was on our side: we were in view of checkout. *I* surrendered to the adrenalin rush, but why couldn't the rest of the troops?

Like us, hundreds of other Londoners on this Saturday were shopping. Concessions were swarming with people of every nationality. I realized how differences melted away here: the desire to make a home is universal. The basis for IKEA's success crystallized for me like never before. A global city of ten million residents, London had beckoned to people of every background and every walk of life. And it seemed that today, they were all here at this particular IKEA trying to find their way home too.

Since there was nowhere to sit with our food, we joined other bedraggled shoppers who'd dropped to the floor propping up against any available anything to rest our IKEA-maxed selves. Consistent with the day, the shuttle back to the train station was leaving just as we hobbled up and we waited for thirty minutes before it returned. Once the shuttle pulled up, I probably don't need to tell you that the driver was due for his coffee-bathroom break. I believe he dilly-dallied.

A cotton-candy vendor was serendipitously strolling

around where we were holding vigil and we weakly caved to the kids' tugging. Two, please. Naturally a parent would want their child to have cotton candy to polish off a meal of Cokes, hotdogs and fries.

The train ride back home was blessedly quiet. I was numbly exalting in our conquest and praising the kids for their great work. "We don't ever want to go back to that place," they mumbled. My husband just looked weary—and relieved. I was completely wasted as well, and feeling contrite. Because of me, it had been a horrible day in the life of our family. A precious Saturday, relegated into the family brain's memory file titled, *Never Again*.

But the mission was over and I had the goods. I'd won. Or had I?

What I had considered to be living up to my responsibilities turned something positive—my energy to create a home—into a tense family crisis.

Guilt flooded me, drowning out any smug satisfaction for having accomplished my mission. Seeing cheer restored to my nearest and dearest would have been well worth surrendering all that I'd materially gained that day. Confronting my pride, I now ached to take the entire day back in exchange for our normally unified family.

Specifically, I had replaced my most valuable asset—my husband—with a handful of notecards.

One of the things that attracted me to my husband both when we first met and to this day is his sense of intuition. It has kept us from doing too much—and too little. It has kept us laughing amidst big adventures that many people would regard warily as too risky. It has kept me from charging when I should proceed with caution just as it has counseled me to charge instead of walk timidly. Over the years, I'd mostly relied on this tremendous secret weapon for guidance.

That day at IKEA I gave ear to my notecards instead of my husband's good judgment. It was a poor decision, considering that it completely made my husband irrelevant. Ruled by my notecards, this negatively executed day was pitted in sharp relief against the best decision I've ever made: the man I chose to marry.

This new me on a new day was no good. Sometimes, conceding defeat is the victory.

Salvation was mine when I unclenched my fist and released what I had wrongly regarded to be victory. My trusty notecards, now represented by the ample stash of small boxes and bulky-papered packages around us on the train, had deluded me. My best friend in battle had been my greatest foe all along.

Walking slowly home from the tube stop to our empty flat, we arrived hand-in-hand, fully reconciled. My husband's run to the grocery for dinner via one of the numerous pubs nearby brought him back refreshed, eyes alive with stories about our new neighborhood.

Not only had my husband forgiven me, he'd already forgotten the lousy day at IKEA. He was the battle-weary but resilient hero. My wounds were more complicated and I was slower to forgive myself, put the day behind me and not further punish the family by treating the IKEA merchandise as contaminated goods. They were simply means to an end, not joys in and of themselves. It had been a remarkably full day in ways I couldn't have predicted.

Our little London flat was alive and buzzing with laughter that night. We unpacked our merchandise side by side as the kids danced around us, as eager as we were to mark this new place as our home. In every way, the grim day at IKEA as well as the intimate living room scene were equally significant in this comprehensive picture; its totality reflected not only the nitty-gritty of moving with young kids, but of marriage.

And my pile of notecards? I let go. They've moved into their new home—the IKEA trashcan.

Sun Worshipers
Olga Mecking

My mom is a professor of genetics and each summer while I was growing up, she was invited to speak at the Biotechnology Summer School that usually took place somewhere along the Polish seaside. At first, my father, a professor of theoretical physics, would tag along as "my mom's husband", but soon he came into his own and suggested some activities he could do with the students. He held a lecture in statistics and then led an expedition to see two sunsets in one day.

For that to happen, you need the sun to set directly over the sea. There can't be any clouds on the horizon. Then you lie down in the sand and watch the sun set. The moment it disappears, you stand up to watch the sun set for the second time. Apparently this can somehow be used to measure the Earth's radius but don't ask me how. I have no idea.

To the onlooker, it must have looked really strange: a group of people simultaneously lying down and then getting up, while intently gazing at the sun. Like a cult: The Sun Worshiper Sect.

Poland isn't the sunniest place in the world, but I always took sunshine for granted. Rainy summers were an exception to the usually warm weather and sunny skies. Even winters had plenty of sunshine, amplified by the snow.

It was only when I moved to the Netherlands that I realized how nice it was in Poland to have four very distinct seasons: cold winters, hot summers, rainy falls and mild springs. The Netherlands has two seasons: rainy and not rainy. But while in some countries these two are distinct— think of monsoons in India—in the Netherlands you can't know where one season ends and the other one begins.

Sometimes you get all kinds of weather—rain, snow, hail, sunshine and a storm—in one single day. That made us change our definition of good weather: it's not the presence of sunshine, but the absence of rain.

Therefore the Dutch are obsessed with sunshine and the outdoors. You know winters are really harsh when the Dutch are forced to get off their bike and push it in front of them. But as long as the weather conditions allow (and I use the word "allow" in a very broad sense), they cycle everywhere.

And expats follow suit. A friend told me that her family and friends were very surprised when they came to visit and found that everything was organized around going outside. We've also become very Dutch in this regard: we use weather apps such as *Buienradar* with great abandon and you will hear us say things like: "It's going to rain now, but in an hour we can go out," or "We need to go out now because it's going to rain in two hours!" The app doesn't always predict the weather perfectly but it's surprisingly accurate.

Ice-skating is another favorite Dutch pastime. When the

winters are cold enough and the ice on the canals is hard and sturdy, the Dutch attempt something called the *Elfstedentocht*—a way to ice-skate through eleven beautiful Dutch cities.

When I first came to the Netherlands in 2009, we had a few cold and snowy winters. I was looking forward to sledding with the kids but in the end, it proved too much hassle to get them dressed into their warm snowsuits and to remember which gloves and hats and scarves belonged to which child.

I have a picture in which I push the stroller during the winter and there's snow everywhere. What I'm walking on is not a street, but a frozen canal. The Netherlands is full of picturesque canals and when the winters are cold enough, they freeze and everyone goes out to ice skate on them or do exactly what I was doing—push the stroller.

How I laughed when a while later my eldest daughter and I were watching a Polish kids' show on YouTube and they specifically warned against doing just that. They are right, of course: safety is paramount. But I think if you see Dutch people out on the frozen canals, you can pretty much assume that they know what they're doing. Besides, my husband wasn't afraid as he used to play ice hockey on frozen lakes growing up.

However, with global warming, winters in the past few years have become increasingly mild. My kids have seen the snow but never in such quantities as I have during my childhood. It's snowing less, raining more during the winter. And temperatures can fall and go up by ten centigrade during one day.

The weather is very unpredictable but the Dutch are prepared. Like sunflowers, they follow the sun when it finally decides to make an appearance and they go out in masses.

You will see them on their bikes. You will see them in cafes under the special heated tents that they build to give the customers the feeling of "being outside." When the canals freeze, they take out their ice skates and go out.

And somewhere, among them, you will see us too. We haven't adapted many other Dutch traditions—I still can't bring myself to celebrate *Sinterklaas*—but we definitely became sun worshipers, like the Dutch.

A Paris Job Ain't All Macarons
Lizzie Harwood

I moved to Paris in May 1999 for a strange gig of baby-sitting a gigantic mansion. There were no office politics because *I* alone was 'the office.' The only other employees in sight were maids and security guys.

So it was a shock, a few years later, to work in an international law firm with over 300 people in the Paris office. The office was too big to greet co-workers by *bise* (air cheek kiss) and too hierarchical to *bise* anyone at all. This was a world where partners ruled and the rest of us supported them. By then, I thought I'd figured out Paris and France, more or less, by virtue of sticking around and taking French classes at Alliance Française. But nope, I hadn't.

I still hadn't twigged to a myriad of customs and cultural differences. I was only ankle deep in terms of *getting* France.

One of the 'perks' of the law firm job was seeing a doctor for the *visite médicale*: an annual health check-up. How kind, it was considered, to ensure staff didn't develop lung cancer from the partners who still smoked inside their office, or rheumatoid arthritis from the typing workload. It was an invitation to play hooky reserved for the worker bees: secretaries and assistants and paralegals and such. Appointments were duly meted out by someone in HR and we were authorized to abandon our desks and take the metro to an address in the sixteenth *arrondissement*—to one of those impressive Haussmann-style buildings with a stone façade, russet-carpeted entrance, and polished brass doorknobs.

I climbed the stairs, figuring I should warm-up for the impending health check, who knew what awaited me? They might have a treadmill and heart beat monitor. This being France, I figured I'd be made to 'perform' in some way. A non-descript receptionist logged in my presence and directed me swiftly into a 'waiting stall'—no, not a waiting room, but an actual stall like cows hang out in for milking, with an 'IN' door leading straight back to Reception and an 'OUT' door leading who knew where.

"*Deshabillez-vous et attendez le médecin.*"

The receptionist kept a grip on my paperwork and shut me into the stall.

Undress and wait for the doctor.

Fine, but wait, no paper robe or other vestige of dignity was in my stall with me. How undressed is 'undressed'? I slowly peeled off my boots, mocha brown stockings, A-line skirt, white shirt... dimly hearing someone exit their stall further along.

The stalls were constructed out of cheap plywood and sported a horrendous salmon paint job. A poster describing sexually transmitted diseases graced one wall, while the other urged you to talk about your gout issues with an image of a guy's feet in bed—one foot transformed into a big pulsating cactus of pain. Who has gout these days? How long would I wait in this stall?

Undress and wait.

I was mid-debate on how much of myself to undress. Underwear on or off? I flicked off my bra, then my *culotte*, folding everything up neatly. Why fold my clothes neatly? Because this was taking ages and in that stall I felt like an unwelcomed temporary resident of France. I sat gingerly, on the wooden bench wondering if I should put the underwear back on. I stewed with resentment for my stupid office job with this unwanted mission. It was—like many aspects of France in my five years there so far—obscure, operating on a need-to-know basis, and just weird.

Oh and it was chilly in that stall. I imagined all sorts of negative repercussions from this naked work-time excursion in November. They certainly hadn't cranked the heating up in this cool stone prison… Pneumonia, I imagined. Maybe crabs from the wooden bench, for another. Clinical depression, why not.

It was yet another flaming hoop to jump through to *fit in* here. I grew up in New Zealand—and even there my six siblings and I didn't exactly *fit in* seamlessly because our parents moved there from Canada. And dad moved to Canada from England at the age of five. We were expat expats, so 'ex'ed from our 'pat' that we didn't know where our 'pat' was, but the three passports we could legally hold came to represent more to us than having one home country. That's why moving to France had seemed normal to me in the first place: it was in our Harwood DNA to shift countries and live somewhere foreign for as long as we felt like it. All experimental expat forays were *au fait* with us.

The 'OUT' door abruptly swung open with a male doctor calling me through. He gestured for me to take a seat. Take a seat before his desk. No hygienic paper in sight, folks.

I sat, shivering by now and hyper aware that my nipples stood to attention, on his visitor's bucket seat answering his medical history inquisition—buck naked and really stressed about picking up genital warts, lice or herpes off his chair.

Then he took my blood pressure and weighed me.

No part of his check-up required me to be undressed.

I'd completely fallen for the receptionist's terse instruction and my nakedness was for nothing. The doctor made no comment about how *deshabillée* I was, and I wasn't sure if I should have been thankful for that or fucking furious. There was no, "Hey whoa, let's back things up and cover up your tushie, Madame!" No, "Oh, geez, that receptionist of mine has zero communication skills, I'm so sorry you were led to believe you'd better unleash your girls just for this poxy, bullshit medical check-up!! Christelle, get this woman her clothes and her dignity!"

No, of course not, because in France embarrassment is not brought out into the open and apologized for, it's ignored. When authority figures make a mistake—it's suddenly invisible. So my nakedness became invisible. He didn't explain or take responsibility; he simply didn't see my tits and vagina perched in his line of vision.

And, you know, it wasn't that I misunderstood the receptionist's words. *Undress and wait* isn't hard to decipher. It was that worker bees in a large French company clearly shouldn't mind sitting buck naked to answer queries on whether they suffer backache or experienced RSI.

"Nope, mister, I don't have backache, I have acute IhatefuckingFrance syndrome right now. Plus Stockholm syndrome probably because I won't even go back to the office and have a fit about this. I'll slink off, put my clothes back on and feel embarrassed. And probably grab a *macaron* on my way to compensate."

On my return trip, I felt enlightened in that awful way of seeing through a curtain you really didn't want to look behind. I reframed the humiliation as all my own perception. Obviously I hadn't hung out in enough European saunas or hammans or gone topless on French beaches to break through my innate queasiness at displaying my body to a total stranger. Perhaps it was the weigh in, maybe French women preferred to be naked so they wouldn't have the weight of their clothing included on their file?

Back at my desk, I made a start on the next monster document to edit and amend, muttering to my cubicle buddies how horrible my check-up was. "They said get undressed, so I did! What the hell."

My French colleague shrugged commiserations, while my Irish colleague growled, "I never take anything off, fuck 'em."

Every subsequent check-up, until I left the job in 2008, I went with the Irish approach. The doctor never commented either way. The receptionist dished out the same terse order, and I learned something—if you don't like the local customs, it's better to pull the 'foreign card' and pretend you don't know what they want from you, rather than argue your point that what they want from you seems stupid and bizarre. It's okay to be a square peg rather than try to shed layers to fit into a round hole. And who cares if your weight includes clothes?

You don't have to be naked to discuss your RSI. Unless you want to…

Africa

Diary of a Mom in Congo
Cecile Dash

May 2013. I arrive home from work and there they are. My husband and two children are waiting for me as I enter the house trying to hold back my tears. "Happy retirement, Mom!" I am thirty-two years old and I quit my job because we are packing up our stuff and moving to… Congo of all places! So I 'retired' from my career to start a new one, as an expat mom, living in the Republic of Congo.

September 2013. OMG… WHAT HAVE I DONE!?! As I sit on the balcony of our hotel room on the sixth floor of the Atlantic Palace Hotel in the Republic of Congo, I am overwhelmed by the traveling, with twelve suitcases and two tired children. I am emotional, and I am scared! *"Don't worry babe, I booked us a VIP arrival when we get there!"* So yes, we got here, Pointe Noire to be exact, and there is this pink building, which I learn is the actual airport. Most passengers turn left but no, not us since my husband booked us the 'VIP arrival,' whatever that means. We get to go straight ahead into a room that for some odd reason has so many couches and lounge chairs in it that it is challenging to get through with our hand luggage and a stroller. At the end of the room is a desk and a very big Congolese man who looks very intimidating. He demands to see our documents and whilst I am on the verge of crying, my husband is extremely nonchalant about the whole thing. After showing our documents to another man at a different desk and another… well you get it, we finally make it to the VIP waiting area.

My husband goes to get our luggage while I wait with the children. I nod and see him off, not realizing that I am on my own with my children, in Congo. This suddenly hits me and I start to cry and try to hide my face. This emotional moment only lasts for maybe two minutes as I see we are now in great danger. There is a mosquito flying around my daughter! As you might know mosquitoes carry malaria and whatever other diseases so I am losing my cool trying to save my daughter's life, which is impossible because these are very special, skilled mosquitoes. As soon as you try to kill them they become invisible, and they make no sound! After what feels like hours of me waiting (in reality maybe thirty minutes), my husband returns and we are taken to our hotel.

The heat, the smell of burning garbage, the buildings, the sound, the people, and the traffic are unlike anything I have ever seen before. OMG rebels. I see rebels! Or, not? Surely all these Toyota pickups filled with Congolese men must be rebels? Are we safe here? I feel so naive for coming here and thinking it would be an adventure!

So here I am on my balcony feeling so incredibly stupid for giving up our life to start a new one. Shit!! This was wrong. We made a mistake. I need to call the moving company. They need to send our container back. I MADE A MISTAKE! Or, not?

I know one person here, actually only via e-mail, and I know that she knows more expat people. So, if they can do it, why can't I? I just have to meet them all... NOW so they can reassure me that things will be okay!

October 2013. We are living in our house in a neighborhood called Tchikobo. I will later learn this is the Beverly Hills of Congo. All of our 'stuff' has arrived. Too much stuff, stuff I feel guilty for having in a country as poor as this. I never really thought we had that much stuff, but I was able to fill up a forty-foot container, aka my whole life in 266 boxes. I was shocked!

My maid (YES I HAVE A MAID) is helping me unpack. As we do not know each other very well and there is a language barrier it is hard to communicate, but she seems very nice. We pay her a fair wage for Congolese standards. After researching salaries a little, I believe I now understand the 'ranking': first you have the drivers they get paid around 350 USD a month. Then you have the *nounous* (nannies) and *menageres* (maids) who make between 200 and 400 USD a month. Lastly, the security guards, gardeners, and pool guys who make between 120 and 200 USD a month. Shocking, right? Every expat has their way of helping their staff as a 'project.' Whether you pay for an operation, medicines, give them a bonus, or pay for their children's school fees, we all try to pay off our guilt by helping. Well, at least I am. Then you also have the occasional weddings and funerals and they will come and tell you about these events. They will clarify that is it custom to give them money for these events, if they notice a blank stare. The best moneymaker by far is the "I am going to name my child after you," because that way you feel honored and responsible, which is the perfect mix to keep giving. Before we travel all the staff know, without us mentioning it, and we get requests for items, mainly electronics, to be brought back for them. My gardener hardly speaks a word to me, but whenever we are about to leave the country he hands me a list: 2x computers, 1x iPad, etcetera. I feel extremely pressured to bring him back something and am amazed that he feels no shame in asking me for these items. Needless to say I have a hard time refusing all their requests and at the same time am a little annoyed as they seem so ungrateful. I read a novel, *The Poisonwood Bible*, where it explains that the Congolese are very skilled at survival. This is what they are doing. Surviving. If it were me, would I hesitate to ask?

As we continue to unpack, my maid is trying not to roll her eyes as I am also explaining what else I expect from her. I made a schedule with tasks for her including my daughter's naps and fruit snacks, etc. By looking at her she obviously thinks I'm crazy.

Okay fine, she has a point, and soon I will let go of my very well organized Excel spreadsheet. She is pushing me though by not really sticking to any of the naptimes and instead carries my daughter on her back all day using my shawls. Remind me why I took my shawls to a country as hot as Congo? Well, we were moving so I have everything here now, including our ski-gear.

December 2013. THE ARTICLE. Someone on Facebook has tagged all of us expat woman into this article about the "9 Different Types of Expats." At first, we all find this hilarious and keep talking about how true this article is and yes of course we know all these different types of expats. Until I get home and read it again and wonder which one I am. I would like to be this one type, but do the others see me like that too? Or, am I the bossy one? I know I can be bossy sometimes. Or… shit, do they think I'm the know-it-all? I am not the only one struggling with this article, as everyone seems to be on their best behavior to fit into the one type that they so desire to be. Nobody wants to be the "Moaning Milly" character, so whereas we would normally end our days complaining about the heat, or the groceries that weren't in the stores, everybody seems awfully happy and interested in how the others are doing! This lasts for about a week until it stops showing up on everyone's feed so we can move on. Pffff, that was exhausting! Back to being bossy and complaining then.

February 2014. As my son climbs out of the pool I see that the pool light floats in the water with some wires still attached to the wall. Again, DANGER! I call the general number we were given for a company that deals with all things in-and-around the house. I tell them to come immediately as this is a very dangerous situation and I do not want anyone to electrocute themselves in my pool. "Sure, Madame (yes, they all call me Madame or Maman) we will come tomorrow!"

"No, not tomorrow… NOW! I NEED YOU NOW PLEASE!" But the man has hung up already. Okay, so I will guard the pool until tomorrow then! When they arrive, eight men to be precise, they are all staring at the pool. They look a bit worried as there is no way they can fix this without getting wet, and I have a feeling they can't swim. So they start to drain the pool. By draining the pool they are now flooding half of the neighborhood I live in! This takes at least four hours and in the meantime they are napping, all eight of them, in my backyard! No. This is unacceptable, I have to go out there and say something.

Rookie mistake—I now know they all sleep a lot, and really anywhere. After I google-translate what I want to say, I go out there and suggest that two people should be more than capable of doing this job. Eight pairs of eyes stare at me. Blankly. I get no reaction... oh wait, some are rolling their eyes, which translates to me as: *Leave us alone we do this, you deal with your house or whatever it is you do!* By 4 p.m. they have screwed the light back to the wall and a truck full of drinking water has just pulled up in front of my house! ARE YOU FILLING UP MY POOL WITH DRINKING WATER???

Yes this is exactly what they are doing! I want to scream now. Why not use tap water? Sure it contains cholera every now and then but we have chlorine tablets. There are so many people here that could use clean drinking water! I now wish I had never called them to begin with. I should have done it myself! What a waste! And a typical example of that saying us expats like to use: TIA (This Is Africa).

March 2014. My daughter walks in the house and says: "*Mbote*, Mom!" Uhh what? My three-year-old daughter is trying to tackle three languages as I am Dutch, my husband is Canadian, and we are sending them to a French school. However "*Mbote*" doesn't fit in any of these three languages. She is picking up the local language now! Spending time with our maid, our guards, our gardener and the pool-man means they have taught her some Lingala! I was already having a hard time understanding her, as my French is not great and she is picking up more French every day, but this has made it even worse. "*Mbote*" means "hello" in Lingala, one of the local languages the Congolese speak.

April 2015. Yeeeyy we are going on another adventure to explore Congo as we set off with three families to a National Park for the weekend. Jungle time! Packed with coolers, water tanks, extra gas and lots of food, we leave on a Friday at noon. The drive there should take us four hours. After the first hour the road sort of ends, but we continue on gravel, sand, and dirt roads. Still very excited about our weekend ahead. After two hours we arrive at something. I think it's a ferry, although this doesn't represent any ferry that I have ever seen before. This sort of floating thing is supposed to take the cars and us across the river. But all is well; we make it across the river in two trips and continue our journey through what already feels like the jungle.

Our air-conditioning stops working in the car. Opening windows is not really an option with the amount of bugs and sand dust flying around. The lady from the park is getting a bit agitated telling us we need to hurry up as apparently we are driving too slowly. After one of the other cars is stuck not once, not twice, but at least three times, we have to stop and pull them out. Our journey takes us a little longer than the estimated four hours. We arrive seven hours later, happy to finally get out of the cars and to see the 'house' we will be staying in for the weekend. As we are standing there I feel mosquitoes eating us alive, so we quickly put mosquito repellent on all the children and ourselves. The house is very basic, only a few hours a day of electricity provided by the generator and no AC. My husband doesn't function without AC, so this will be challenging.

Once we decide where everybody will sleep we make the beds and cook dinner. This is almost impossible with the heat. I'm trying my best to be excited, but I am feeling too hot to do anything! There are bugs everywhere in the house and when I step outside I feel even more bugs, but lucky for me it's too dark to identify what they look like. I think it is safe to say that none of us, six adults and seven children, had any sleep that night and are super excited when the sun rises and we can get up! The highlight so far would be the cold shower, for sure!

We are going on a morning safari at 6 a.m. and most of the children fall asleep during this very bumpy drive. I enjoy the beautiful ride and am truly happy with the decision we made to move to Congo. Later that day we enter the jungle by boat and again have an amazing experience. We even saw a wild elephant! My children were of course asleep again for this experience. Our planned BBQ is challenging to say the least because of so many bugs and mosquitoes. At this point I don't even want to talk to anyone anymore. I'm too tired and too hot! We have put seven children in front of one iPad and hope that the battery will last as we have no means to charge it. As I am taking another cold shower I see that my nail polish has been eaten by the amount of Deet I have been putting on my children. Let's hope we can sleep tonight as everyone is exhausted and we are all in bed before 9 p.m. Noooo, someone is snoring! As it is an open-plan house this is extremely annoying. Shortly after two of the kids start crying (one of them is mine so no complaints here).

Finally it is sort of quiet until my husband jumps up screaming. I quickly grab my phone and shine my flashlight on him. EEEIIIUUUWWWW! This must be the biggest cockroach I have ever seen! And it's on his face! I'm trying not to laugh as he is visibly upset. The next morning my favorite part of the day again is my cold shower. This time I am accompanied by rat poop in the shower, but I don't care anymore! I have left out many details such as the maggots in our meat, the fridge that didn't work, etc., etc.

We are all very happy to go home and my romantic ideas of a trip to the jungle have been crushed. We were already friends with the other two couples, but this trip has bonded us for life!

May 2015. My husband calls me from work on a Friday morning to tell me he is not feeling well and is going to the clinic to get tested for malaria. This is nothing special as we live in a country where there is malaria. He comes back saying the test was negative, but he does have a throat infection. On Saturday he feels worse and his temperature keeps spiking up to 40°C degrees. We have malaria test kits at home and I do another one, but again the result is negative. I'm already getting a little annoyed dealing with the children by myself and him lying in bed having a typical case of man-flu. Sunday morning, he's not making much sense and now I'm getting worried, as all the paracetamol still hasn't reduced his fever. I do another test on him and almost throw it away assuming it's negative again. But it isn't. It came back positive! I call a friend to look after my children and we rush to the clinic.

There are many different types of malaria, and it turns out my husband has a very serious case. He stays in the hospital for over a week and almost needs a blood transfusion—something you don't want done in Congo. Later on that week the doctor confessed to me that he didn't think my husband was going to make it, as the parasite count in his blood was extremely high. At the time I did not realize the situation was that bad.

After the first day in the hospital I go home to pick up some clothes and toiletries for my husband, I find two schedules on the door of the fridge. One schedule was for food. Yes, food! My friend informed the rest of our extended expat-family that my husband was in the hospital. So they did what a family would do. They look after each other.

Here I am in Congo feeling tired and upset, and I see these two schedules. My friends communicated among each other about who would cook meals/snacks for the next week for my husband, the children, and me. The other schedule was who was looking after the children, doing school pickups, and play dates. (CAN YOU BELIEVE THAT?)

This is what makes expat life special. You are all in this adventure together. We've all left behind our families. We all understand what you go through because we have all been there. During this horrible time, I realized that while being skeptical of becoming an expat mom I never in a million years would have thought it could be this great. And if you were able to organize a move to a different country with your family, you have already moved up on my list as this is hard, emotional, stressful, and requires some serious organizational skills!

Being part of an expat community keeps me sane while living in a country so different from the one I grew up in. It makes up for the hassle of trying to find groceries, dealing with all of the power cuts, the corrupt police, the lack of high-speed Internet, the many strange, weird bugs my children have gotten over the years, the language barriers, the cultural differences, and so much more! They become your family and you share things with them that bond you forever, the good and the bad.

So, this is our adventure that started almost three years ago. When we arrive at the pink airport these days, I find it difficult to imagine how terrified and intimidated I was of this building the very first time. Reliving it now it feels like a lifetime ago, as this is now our home. It's a place where I feel safe and happy. A place where I have grown so much as a person and above all, a place that I truly love and hate at the same time!

...By the way, my husband got his malaria from our little trip to the jungle.

Lost in Libya
Lesley-Anne Price

After spending a year in Italy, which could only be described as heavenly, our next posting was going to be Libya. I think it's fair to say that I was quite shocked when my husband came home with the 'not so good news'. At the time I was pregnant with our first child and was very happy living *la dolce vita*. Not only was I gutted to be leaving *bella Italia*, but I also had some serious reservations about going to Libya. Libya was a country that I knew very little about. The little I did know about it, was not good: the Lockerbie connection and that 'mad dog' dictator, Colonel Gaddafi. As well as my ignorance about the country, I had never met any Libyans before in my life and so I was quite concerned and feeling somewhat apprehensive about the new posting. However, as daunting as it was, I decided to look on it as a new adventure.

So when Andrew was just four months old, we joined my husband for our new adventure in Libya. The timing was fortunate for us, as we could now fly directly to Libya, following the lifting of the UN sanctions which were imposed in retribution for the bombing of PAN AM 103 over Lockerbie. After eight years of economic hardships due to the UN sanctions, I was expecting some hostility and resentment from the Libyan people towards Westerners. The reality was in fact very different. My preconceived notions about the Libyan people were totally unfounded.

From the moment we arrived in Libya, we were made to feel welcome. I was immediately struck by how kind and friendly the people were and how they appeared to be genuinely interested in us. We were warmly greeted by smiling and pleasant people, who talked to us in English. A favourite phrase which we heard a lot was, 'Welcome to Libya'. And having a gorgeous baby boy also ensured we attracted our fair share of attention.

As we drove from the airport, my first impression of Libya was that the landscape was very sandy and barren, dotted with occasional palm trees. The other most striking thing as we drove through the dusty streets of Tripoli, was that it seemed to be a country full of men. I wondered to myself, 'Where are all the women?'

It turned out that during the day it was unusual to see Libyan women. It was men who worked in the shops, businesses, market stalls and the souk. It was very strange at first and took some getting used to, especially being served by a man in the ladies' lingerie shop! However, as day turned to night groups of women would take to the streets chatting and laughing as they went about their business and did their shopping. During the day most Libyan women were busy at home, doing the cooking and the cleaning and looking after young children. It was during the evenings that Libyan women would have the opportunity to escape the confines of the home.

Libya was quite a moderate Muslim country under

Gaddafi's dictatorship. He had actively suppressed any forms of Islamic extremism. Despite some degree of tolerance, there were nonetheless still some strict social rules and cultural norms, for example keeping young males and females separate. It was common to see all male and all female groups but you wouldn't see any mixed groups. You would never see courting couples and public displays of affection between the sexes was forbidden. When we were still new to Libya and unaware of all the rules, my husband and I had inadvertently caused a bit of a stir during a furniture shopping trip. A company driver accompanied us and on returning to the office, one of my husband's colleagues tactfully informed him that it wasn't socially acceptable to give his wife a peck on the cheek in public. Even holding hands was frowned upon.

During our early days in Libya, some of my husband's Libyan colleagues would come round to the house in the evenings. But they would never sit in the living room with my baby and me; instead they would sit outside on the veranda. They weren't being unfriendly; it just wasn't normal or acceptable for them to mix with women socially. They would always greet me first and in typical Libyan style would ask me how I was, how was the baby, the rest of my family, etc. Libyan greetings could go on forever by the time they had checked on your well being and that of all your family members. The Libyans were very family-oriented people.

The Libyans loved children and were especially fond of children with north European looks. Our son Andrew, with his blond hair and blue eyes always attracted a lot of attention and being a boy made him even more special. The Libyans would often kiss your babies and young children. Complete strangers would even try to take your baby from your arms or prise him or her from their pushchair. It was quite alarming at first but you soon got used to it and became prepared for it whenever you went out.

Our second child, Kristina, was born in Libya and our third one, Katherine, was born in Malta, a forty-minute plane ride away. All three of our children were repeatedly kissed and fussed over wherever we went. Whenever I took them shopping, I would often find somebody had slipped them a lollipop or some sweets without me realising. Although there was a part of me that felt annoyed by this, at the same time I realised that it was done in good nature and just learnt to accept it as a gesture of kindness.

The driving in Libya was a nightmare! The rules of the road were 'there are no rules' and you soon learnt to expect just about anything. The Libyans had an Inshallah attitude when it came to driving. It was all down to God's will whether you got from A to B in one piece!

There was a huge roundabout in Tripoli, which was aptly named and commonly referred to as 'Death Roundabout'. It was completely chaotic and did not follow any normal 'roundabout rules', with drivers even going the wrong way in order to take the shortest route! It was the main roundabout as you entered the city centre and almost impossible to avoid. Fortunately we always made it out alive! Libya used to be an Italian colony and the standing joke among the expats was that the Italians taught the Libyans how to drive. Even my Italian friends would joke about it!

Initially we only had one car, which my husband used for work. After our second child was born, we hired a part-time driver, a slightly elderly and very affable man who had previously worked for my husband's company. Unfortunately his driving skills were a bit shoddy and to make matters worse, he was blind in one eye. After many eventful driving episodes and near misses with pedestrians and other cars, I managed to persuade my husband to buy another car so I could drive myself. Although the driving was pretty scary at first, I soon got used to it and at least my children were with a careful and safe driver. In a strange way, I grew to enjoy the challenge and the adrenaline rush you got from driving along the crazy streets of Tripoli.

Apart from the general chaos, lawlessness and craziness on the roads, in the days before GPS another hurdle was that it was very easy to get lost. On one such memorable occasion, I had been visiting a friend who lived in another camp on the other side of the city and had managed to get well and truly lost on my way back to pick up my son from school.

Tripoli could be very disorientating, as much of it looked pretty much the same and there were very few distinguishing landmarks. Also the road signs were all, of course, in Arabic, which I didn't understand. Back in those days I didn't have a mobile phone, so I couldn't even phone anybody to try to get some help. With my two year old daughter, fortunately, blissfully fast asleep in her car seat in the back, I was driving round in circles and up and down unfamiliar stretches of road trying unsuccessfully to get my bearings. To make matters worse, some crazy guy was following me and he kept driving past, grinning madly and gesturing. Just my luck, not only had I managed to get myself totally lost but was also being stalked by some crazy fruit loop!

After I eventually managed to lose my stalker, I decided to pull over next to a row of garages. By this time I was feeling quite panicky and stressed as it was getting closer to my son's school pickup time. Despite feeling very vulnerable and helpless, I needed to do something. I noticed a group of men who were standing outside one of the garages. So I got out of my car and nervously approached the men asking, 'Excuse me, does anybody speak English?' They all turned round and stared at me, before one of them answered, 'Yes I do.' I explained to him that I was lost and that I needed to find my way to the British School to pick up my son. He explained directions to the school, but he could clearly tell from my blank expression that I didn't have a clue! So he said something to his friends in Arabic and then said, 'Come on follow me, I'll show you the way.'

I quickly got back into my car and started to follow him, desperately trying not to lose him on the way. I realised that I was taking a big risk by following a stranger through an unfamiliar part of town, but I decided to trust my instincts and go with it. Fortunately the risk paid off and sure enough, he led me to my son's school. When we arrived at the school I got out of my car and thanked the man and offered him some money, at least to pay for his petrol I explained, if nothing else. But he refused to take any money; instead he shook my hand and wished me well before driving away.

Needless to say, I was extremely relieved and thankful that I'd made it back to the school and on time to pick up my son. My daughter, Kristina, was still fast asleep and completely oblivious to what had been going on during the last couple of hours. That incident really restored my faith in humanity and showed me once again how genuinely kind the Libyans could be.

Whenever I mention to people that we spent five years in Libya, the usual response is, 'Oh!' followed by silence or sometimes, 'What was that like?' I respond by telling them how much I enjoyed our time in Libya and I mention all the good things about it: the beautiful unspoilt beaches and swimming in the Mediterranean Sea with my children, the day trips to the amazing Roman ruins of Leptis Magna and Sabratha, the souk, the kind and friendly people and the favourable climate (apart from the hottest summer months). I look back on those years with much fondness and some nostalgia.

For Libya, it was an exciting time of change and opportunity as the country was opening up again to foreign investment, following the years of sanctions and economic hardships. Despite the fact that the shops, restaurants and other amenities were basic, we made the most of what we had. We made a lot of good friends there and we enjoyed lots of fun and memorable times together. For me, those years will always hold a special place in my heart, because that's where I spent the first five years of motherhood and that was where I began the journey of raising my three lovely children. With much sadness, I have watched events unfolding in Libya in recent years. I have been utterly dismayed by the chaos, lawlessness and the destruction that the country has fallen into. It's heartbreaking to watch a country with so much potential and such rich natural resources slide into ruin. I truly hope that Libya will find some peace and stability one day soon.

An Unbelievable Bus Ride
Camille Armantrout

I don't care what anyone says, travel is not glamorous. Especially not in Sub-Saharan Africa. Certainly there can be great moments; as in a short first-class flight involving brie or a linen-napkin dining car meal through the Swiss Alps. But for the most part, travel involves queues, cramped spaces, and long hours of sitting. Travel demands humility, patience, resistance to heat and cold, and excellent bowel and bladder control.

My husband Bob, our grown daughter Amy and our friend Dave had just spent a week in northern Ghana at Tamale, and at Mole National Park mingling with wild African elephants. One morning we returned from safari to decimated shrubbery and elephantine footprints. While we were out stalking elephants, a pair of them had been enjoying a snack outside our rooms! Bob had wisely planned the trip at the end of the dry season when animals would be close to the large watering hole below the lodge.

In addition to elephants, we were treated to an inside look at the savanna, an expanse of grassland and shrubs populated with towering termite mounds, spindly acacia trees and the occasional baobab. It was a very different landscape from southern Ghana where we had been living for seven months. Kumasi's trees were tall and lush in comparison, broad-leafed avocado and mango, cocoa, and a wide variety of palms, including royal, traveler's, coconut and oil.

We spent three mornings exploring the park on foot, accompanied by armed rangers. One showed us a rich variety of animals, another pointed out dozens of birds we'd never seen before and a third taught us medicinal uses for savanna plants. Amy, a student of herbal healing eagerly drank in the information. I was impressed by the tree with antibiotic properties and bark, which easily tore into long, supple strips for binding wounds.

Our stay in Tamale gave us a look at a different culture. The streets were clogged with bicycles and scooters whereas in southern Ghana, taxis rule the road. Although we were used to seeing women carrying things on their heads, Tamale was the only place we ever saw a woman riding a bicycle while balancing a head pan of oranges.

Best of all, we spent some time with a fascinating older couple, family friends that Bob knew from his childhood in Ghana forty years before. When Bob was nine his family moved to Ghana, which was one of the main reasons we seized the opportunity to move to Kumasi.

It was a lovely week, and now we were going home.

The digital clock at the front of the bus reads 1:15 a.m. It's 7:15 according to my cell phone and we're already leaving Tamale for Kumasi, 315 kilometers (195 miles) south. The name on the front of the bus is 'Still Believers' and that seems fortuitous. If all goes well, we'll reach home in six hours.

The bus is full so it's time to go. In Ghana, transport

doesn't move without a full load. The driver begins inching forward through the dusty, crowded yard, squeezing past vendors, chickens and taxis in the early morning light.

The four of us are elated. We congratulate ourselves for arriving early and deciding not to wait for the VIP or STC (State Transport Company) buses. We're feeling very clever about choosing a privately owned bus because it was nearly full.

We are making the best of a bad situation. We would have flown had the airport not run out of fuel the day of our departure. Our favorite driver Eric got us to Tamale in a record-breaking, hair-raising five and a half hours. But the planes are still grounded, so we were stuck with the bus.

I make a mental note: When the clock in the front of the bus reads 7:11, we should be in Kumasi. 1:00 our time. 711. One of our favorite numbers. I'm thinking, "This is a lucky day."

An African wearing a bright yellow shirt with a blue plastic rosary around his neck flashes a bright smile when the bus bumps out onto the asphalt. People straddle plastic stools, which have been placed in the center aisle. We are the only *obrunis* (white people) on the bus. Our big blue duffle bag sits atop a motorcycle in the cargo compartment beside a stack of crisp goatskins. The windows are all opened, unlike the air-conditioned VIP buses we leave behind.

A radio plays a chanting song that reminds us of Muslim call to prayer. The man in the yellow tee shirt is reading the Catholic Edition of *The Good News Bible*. A woman a couple of seats forward barks into her cell phone. Amy looks serene. Dave sits in the wide back seat with six or seven Ghanaians. The sun rises steadily into the white sky.

Dodging potholes, the bus lumbers past the Asempa

Lodge where we stayed our first night in Tamale. I scan the yard for the elusive donkey. Bob and I had wandered the courtyard in search of the animal but only found dusty piles of donkey poo, many of which contained excreted plastic bags. All evidence had pointed to death by plastic.

We sit at the first police checkpoint for a while. Moments later *Military Zone*, a stellar example of Nollywood (Nigerian cinema) begins playing on the ancient King Long Flatscreens that hang from the ceiling. The actors are already yelling and pushing each other around. Mercifully, the nearest screen is spoiled (the local term for broken). All we see are a series of flickering blue and yellow lines.

9:15 – Two hours into our trip, they are playing *Military Zone* for the second time and the digital clock at the front of the bus has either fallen out or been removed, leaving a branch of capped electrical wires. They sway with the motion, gently waving at us—a gentle reminder that clocks mean nothing here.

I fill a zip-lock bag with dried fruit, almonds, and a bar of chocolate for Dave. Bob asks the man behind us to pass it back and Dave becomes the envy of the back seat passengers. A baby sits on her mother's lap next to Amy, watching the trees float by.

9:45 – The bus sits on the side of the road. The driver has gotten out. We suspect engine trouble. Passengers are taking advantage of the stop. I recall the conversation we had with a man in the desolate Tamale airport parking lot. Weighing our options, I asked whether any of the buses had toilets. "No," the man chuckled, "But all you have to do is tell the driver and he will stop the bus so you can free yourself." "And why wouldn't he?" I laughed, "Better to stop the bus than have us free ourselves in the aisle."

We followed the others, nabbing a potty break before picnicking in the shade of a small tree. It's tricky, eating in public. We all forgot to wipe with our left hand and there's no place to wash. The Ghanaians assume we use our left in the bush and eat with our right like they do, so we have to be careful not to let them see that we are eating with our left hands.

While we eat, we keep our eyes open for Fulani herdsmen. The Fulanis, cattle rich and cash poor are notorious bandits. And they are armed. People who travel through this part of the country after dark do so in caravans with armed escort. Bob wonders if we will end up sleeping in our tree.

After freeing themselves behind an un-roofed masonry block building, the women file back toward the bus and seat themselves on the shaded asphalt. Most of the men stand in a tight group behind the bus, watching the driver work on the engine. A few others drift out onto the savanna, each choosing a tree to sit in or lean against. A mother nurses her infant. A VIP bus rolls by on its way to Kumasi.

As we mill around the bus, the words 'Still Believers' above the windshield mock us. At this point, we have no other option but to believe that the bus will run again. We admire the decals, leaping tigers, Asian Elvises and 'Rasta Baby' a sleepy-eyed infant with a joint.

A man in bright orange shower shoes (flip flops) walks up the road from another broken bus to join the men clustered around ours. A truck pulls onto the shoulder and several of the men sprint over with five-gallon cans, filling them with water. They cool the engine and replace a belt.

Finally the driver shuts the hatch, climbs into his seat and starts the engine. He says nothing. No words are necessary. Everyone lines up for re-boarding. When the engine roars, we know what to do.

11:11 – We're moving again! The baby naps. Slow conversations murmur through the bus while hot air blows through the open windows. This day is made of endless, timeless moments.

At a junction the bus is engulfed in vendors. "Here wat aah!" "Here wat aah!" calls the woman behind me out her window. A young girl with a pan of sachets on her head hurries over. Cedis are passed through windows in exchange for bananas, buns, and roasted yam. The floor begins to look like a Chinese train. We move on, the bus smelling sweetly of roasted yam and fried buns.

For a few moments we sit again, driverless, engine idling, gazing at the collection of slumbering umbrella vendors on stools beside their racks of cell phone accessories. The driver climbs back in to pilot us a little further down the road. Bob read that this trip can take twelve hours, and we are beginning to understand why.

The women in their bright wraps giggle and chat happily. The young men in the aisles hang onto a seat back as they balance on their cracked plastic stools. I eat a few pieces of boiled potato and drink a can of fruit juice.

1:00 – The sweet smell of cashew trees outside Kintampo. We are whizzing along, sweating in our seats, hoping for the best. Inexplicably, the driver did not call for another bus or a mechanic at the last stop. He probably doesn't want to pay for help. We have no choice but believe in him and his bus. If our luck improves we will reach home in another three hours.

1:05 – Stopped again. The driver pulls onto the shoulder and gets out. Five minutes later, passengers follow suit.

1:35 – Moving again. The women are all worked up. The driver explains he is doing his best. The man with the blue rosary is saying we need to relax. Amy wonders if she should pull out her Kava tincture and offer it to the passengers.

Some left and caught a passing cab at the last breakdown, making their way out of this mess. Bob offered a *tro tro* 200 cedis to take us to Techiman and was turned down. Techiman is now our beacon of hope. It is where we can get another bus as long as we reach before the last one leaves at sundown.

And then, we are broken down again at a desolate crossroads where a woman sells cold-water sachets from a blue cooler. The bus is no longer 'spoiled,' it is 'finished.' It is finally clear that we all need to make other arrangements.

Just as before, the driver pulled over and got out without saying a word. After five minutes or so we begin peering out the windows and eventually get off. The story ripples through the crowd of displaced passengers. It's over and the driver is going to refund our fares. The rest is up to us.

A man crosses the street toward us with some intent. His ankle is chained to a heavy log, which he cradles in his arms. He is agitated, shouting and it quickly becomes apparent we *obrunis* are his target. Amid the gibberish I hear him say he wants to rid the planet of the white people who have made a mess of this world. I'll give him that, I think. "I'm going to kill you," he says menacingly. And then, "I have a gun."

By now the passengers are boarding *tro tros* (passenger vans) and leaving the scene. The madman has retreated to the other side of the road. He reclines in the dust beside his log, eyeing us angrily. He gets up and begins writing anti-*obruni* sentiments with chalk on the mud wall of a house. Amy is taking this in stride. Coward that I am, I'm hiding behind a group of full-bodied women. Bob and Dave tell me not to worry, that they can take this guy. "But the gun!" I say. "He's just bluffing," they assure me.

Another *tro* pulls up, fills with passengers and speeds away toward Techiman. Finally, a taxi stops and agrees to take us. The bus driver refunds us 20 cedis toward the 80 we paid him for this ride to nowhere. We stuff our duffle bag into the trunk of the cab and leave the mad log man behind.

2:45 – We are loaded and flying south in a cushy *tro* named *Mogya Bi Akasa*. I have no idea what that means. This is my first ride ever in a *tro tro*. There are fourteen passengers and a driver. It only cost us 5.50 cedis (US$2.82) each. We buy ice cream before setting off through the heat. The *tro* careens around corners, missing sheep and people. Bob says this driver would give Eric a run for his money.

5:00 – Ten hours after congratulating ourselves on our savvy choice of bus, we reach Kumasi and find a taxi home. Life is good. My belief in our good fortune validated.

Mrs. Matt in West Africa
Sarah Murdock

I married Matt in picturesque Leesburg, Virginia, USA in June 1996, and in September we flew to his home in Benin, West Africa. He had been a missionary in the region for three years already, and I was going to find out how I fit into the picture. I left a developing career and busy social life in Washington, DC, to find myself in a dusty town in the hinterland of the north with few prospects for close friends and no identity of my own. I became simply Mrs. Matt.

I was no stranger to Africa—my father had been in the US Foreign Service, and I had lived in Morocco (where I learned my basic French, indispensable in Benin) and Kenya for six years as a child. But now I was an adult and not a dependent, a missionary and not a diplomat brat, in a rural town and not a large city. I was also a new bride, learning how to set up housekeeping in a strange land. I had a whole new learning curve.

For one thing, I was not prepared for the heat, the inescapable heat! It could get up to 120°F (almost 50°C) and sometimes it did not go below 90°F (32°C) inside the house at night. We did not have air-conditioning, just fans—as long as the electricity was working. I must have spent the first two or three years just trying to figure out how to not be hot and sweaty. Matt kept gently reminding me that focusing on it so much would only make it worse. He was right. I finally stopped complaining, stopped sitting right in front of a fan draped with a wet cloth, or lying on the slightly cool cement floor. But in the worst heat, I did continue to sleep at night with a wet cloth over me, and a bucket next to the bed to re-dip the cloth every thirty minutes or so, as long as I was awake. It helped immensely, even if it did impede my sleep a bit.

I was glad to speak French already; however, it did not help much when I went marketing, because not too many women (the vast majority of market vendors) in Tanguiéta spoke the national language. There are about eight different tribes living in that region, each with a distinct language. There is a trade language of sorts, but not everyone knew it, so I learned their way of sign language to communicate prices of the few offerings. When we first arrived, I was only guaranteed to find tomatoes, onions and garlic in the market. A few other things were available seasonally, such as lemons, mangoes, okra, and green leafy vegetables. Over the years, more varieties made their way to us, including green beans, cabbage, carrots, lettuce and eggplants. It became an adventure to go the market and see what I could find that day, and I felt quite triumphant when I could bring home something a little unusual. Some things, like eggplant, I had never cooked before, but I scooped them up anyway, just because it was something different, and I knew I could figure out what to do with it later. I came to enjoy the seasonal nature of the produce, because it gave us something to look forward to and made each item that much more appreciated.

Everything I brought home (except the onions and garlic and tubers) had to be bleached, including the meat. The beef was sold on a cement slab, covered in flies and indistinguishable as to parts. It was sold as 'with bones' or 'without bones.' The 'without bones' included filet, lungs, liver, stomach and rump meat. I had to learn how to try to politely decline the innards they wanted to give me, in favor of the muscle meat. The 'with bones' was all hacked up with bits of bone chips everywhere. We bought chickens live and butchered them at home. Somewhere on the edge of town, or in a non-Muslim neighborhood, men sold pork meat that was cut up into chunks. Eggs were very risky; I tried the float test, but it was not always reliable and we just had to guess. We quickly learned to appreciate the compliment, "You're a good egg!"

One of the best things about living in Benin was the slower pace of life for me after the rushed pace of Washington. It was slow in a pioneerish way—each day was busy with daily living, which all took much more time without all our modern conveniences. For one thing, I had to make most of our food from scratch. Tacos, a meal that is quick to fix here in the US, would involve me making the tortillas, grinding the beef, making salsa and refried beans (from black eyed peas, the only bean available in the market), grating the cheese, and making yogurt to substitute for sour cream. Needless to say, this dish was reserved for special occasions! But aside from the market, there was really not much to do and nowhere to go, and this was before streaming Internet and DVDs, so our entertainment was extremely simple. We read books, tried to watercolor and learn constellations (but only when there were no malaria-laden mosquitoes out at night), listened to cassettes of old-time radio shows, and played cards. This was before we had three children. After they arrived, things got a lot livelier!

As missionaries, we were on-call 24/7 and never knew when someone would show up at our door with an emergency. Matt had many a late night call to hurry to some village with the pickup truck to get a laboring woman to the hospital (he didn't always make it in time...). Stranded white people would show up after dark looking for a place to stay till morning. Someone might bring a friend or child (always at night, for some reason) who had been bitten by a snake or stung by a scorpion, because we had an electric shock treatment to neutralize the poison. Many of our visitors wanted financial help of some kind. But not all were looking for help. Some were mad at us because we provided refuge for a sister/daughter/niece fleeing a forced marriage, and more than once machete-wielding men came to claim their girls. We were told witch doctors lurked around trying to curse us. Children would show up at the most awkward hours to have their wounds tended. Sometimes we were gratified that we could help, sometimes we were heartsick at how helpless we felt, sometimes we were exasperated that yet another meal was getting interrupted, or that the same person kept coming again and again for help, sometimes we were so tired we wished we could put up a big gate and keep everyone out. No gate would keep people out, though, since we had insisted on building a wall around our property that was only a meter high, and not the standard two meters. We had done that on purpose, so we would not be cut off from our neighbors. It did get wearisome, but in our better moments, we were grateful for the opportunities to help where we were able.

One particularly startling request came one day after we had been in Tanguéta for about two years. A woman from our neighborhood arrived with a young man to serve as her interpreter. She explained that she had had a white child. We speculated that the father had been a European and that the baby was just light skinned. The problem, as she saw it, was that as a white child he would not be able to eat their Beninese cuisine, or participate in the field work that all family members needed to help with, etc. As the conversation continued, we realized that her baby was an albino, and that she was offering us her child. We reassured her that he could eat whatever they did, and live life as they did, and politely declined her offer. Some years later we got to know Michel, and we helped him with sunscreen and sunglasses, and tried to convince him to wear a hat to protect his skin.

The problems facing the local population seemed staggering at times, and we certainly were not there to solve them all, nor was that even possible. But it was wonderful to think that a few things we did made a huge difference. When we first arrived, for example, most everyone we knew ran out of food months before the next harvest was due. That meant that they would not have the energy needed to plant their new crops, which meant less ground cultivated, and of course a resultant smaller crop, and even worse problems the next year. Matt helped the farmers we knew make some simple calculations, such as: total harvest divided by twelve months until next harvest equated to how much they would have to eat per month. After a few years of this, the requests for food largely stopped, unless there was a bad growing season. In addition, I worked with a local midwife to teach women on the importance of *only* breastfeeding their babies for the first year, and the babies we saw went from often being skinny, lethargic and sickly, to being fat and sassy—it was truly amazing.

A wonderful aspect of our life was that whatever we wanted to try, we could, as long as we had enough money (and we always did everything on a shoestring budget). If Matt woke up one morning and decided he would like to try a new way of planting rice, he did. If we wanted to see if donkeys could be raised and used for carts, as they were in the country to the north, we bought donkeys. If we read about a tree that had almost miraculously nutritious leaves, we ordered seeds and planted them. Because lack of protein was a serious issue, I learned how to make tofu from the soybeans they sold in the market, and taught women how to make it. Some projects worked, some didn't, and some were just before their time.

One of the most fun things about living where we did was all of the animals that came our way. In our first year, a man entered our yard with a horse for sale. Matt was from cowboy country in Wyoming and grew up around horses, and I loved to ride, so we bought it on the spot. It mattered not that we had no place to put her, we just tied her under a tree. As for food, she could just eat grass until we found out what else to get her. Eventually we were brought a second horse, and built some mud brick stables for them.

We soon became the go-to destination for hunters who had killed mother animals and found helpless babies they wanted to sell, or for children who wanted to make some easy money by selling us animals. We were brought baby vervet monkeys, a baboon, duikers (small deer), hedgehogs, ducklings, owls, hares, kittens. It was so hard to resist. We did take the duikers (only three survived babyhood), and some of the others, but most died, being just too young to live without their mothers. Eventually we began to decline most of the animals because we didn't want to encourage people to take them out of the bush.

When we married, my husband already had two monkeys. One died before we returned together to Benin, and we began to think of getting another vervet to be a companion for his remaining monkey. He was away on a trip when I got news that there was a baby available in a village not far away. I rode on horseback to go see it. When Matt returned, we went together to get it, again on horseback. It was so young. The trip took longer than we had planned, and on our return it was beginning to get dark and we needed to canter. Matt folded the little guy into his T-shirt and off we went, with the monkey clinging tightly to Matt's stomach. Once home, we knew we had to keep him in the house for a while, till he got bigger. He sat on our laps at meal times and had the run of the place until he became too naughty. We put him to sleep in a basket by the side of our bed, but soon he was not content to stay in it, so we had to turn it over, put him underneath, and weigh it down so he couldn't escape. He came with us on our first anniversary trip to a nearby waterfall and rustic hotel. Eventually we put him outside under the same tree (but opposite side) of our other monkey.

This monkey, Francis, had a propensity to escape from the chained belt around his waist. When he got loose, he terrorized the neighborhood, stealing corn, jumping on thatched roofs, and scaring people. Of the two of us, I was the one he allowed to approach him when he was loose, but Matt was the only one he would allow to touch him, so in order to catch him, we had to work as a team. I could spend a good hour following Francis around the neighborhood from tree to tree, with a spoon, some jam, and some crushed up Valium (available over the counter). Each time I reached a tree he was in, I put some treated jam on the spoon and handed it up to him. He ate it, disdainfully dropped the spoon, and took off again. Matt usually went into the house to work while all this was going on. If I could get Francis back to the compound, once he started to get a little woozy (which took a surprisingly large amount of Valium), I could grab him by the tail. In order to keep from being bitten, however, I had to spin him madly around while yelling at the top of my lungs for Matt to hurry and get him before he got me!

Not all the animals were welcome, however. We did have our share of creepy ones—the various snakes, scorpions, horrible wind scorpions, bats that flew into the house through holes in the roof, and the ubiquitous cockroaches. We killed more than one snake in the house with machetes, and though the children had some encounters with scorpions, thank God no one ever got stung. It's a miracle that for all their barefoot (always barefoot) running around outside through the tall grasses and down trails, they never met any snakes.

Americans sometimes think they are the only ones who think the food other people eat is weird. *Of course they will love our food—it's normal and delicious!* I learned differently! We housed a number of students from villages in the region on our compound so they could attend the local high school, and regularly had them at our table. One once told me, after the fact, that he almost threw up when I served spaghetti and sauce. He had never eaten spaghetti without lots of rice mixed in. Another time I was with a friend, who had invited me to a party in a village not far away. It was afternoon, and the action wouldn't really start for several hours, so we went from hut to hut, alternately visiting her friends and sitting on mats in the shade. At one point, she brought me the roasted hindquarters of a chicken to eat. Yum! After a few bites, I noticed it was a little pink inside, so I told her, "You know, I think I will save the rest for Matt!" (who had not come), and put it in a bag. Later, I shared with her a granola bar that a recent visitor had brought from the US. She took a bite, and then said, "I think I will save the rest for Baba!" (Her husband.) Touché.

Of course, we were expected to eat and drink what we were so generously served. And we couldn't fool people by tipping a gourd to our mouths, just touching the drink to our lips. But we weren't the only ones challenged by this. Once Matt went to a nearby Fulani camp. The Fulani are a nomadic cattle-herding tribe of West Africa, roundly distrusted and disliked by all others, and this family was keeping some cows for us (as I said, my husband comes from cowboy country). Matt took one of the students with him. When they arrived, a woman was milking a cow, squirting the warm, creamy liquid into a dirty, fly-encrusted gourd. Happy to see Matt, she brought over the gourd and had someone fetch last night's leftovers, a thick corn porridge that had sat out uncovered overnight, tasted by who-knows-what insects. She poured the milk into the bowl of porridge and then took her hand and mushed it all together, and smilingly offered it to Matt. The boy with him blanched and said, "I will *not* eat that!" "Oh yes, you will," Matt replied, as he took a nice big gulp and handed it to him.

When we first moved into our first home, we had no running water or electricity hooked up. We did have a telephone, though, and dial-up Internet was actually working for a while, so to power the computer, Matt would drive our pickup truck right up to the front door, leave it running, and hook the computer up to the battery. Telephones were still relatively rare, and sometimes one of the students would ask to use the phone to get a message to his home in another village (usually via the nearest health clinic or police station, the only phones in the village). His friends would come just to watch! Once when we were away, we were delayed on our return and called the house, so we could let someone know. No answer. But later, one of the students asked us whether we had heard him—he said he had been standing outside the window as it rang, yelling at it! We would often get calls late at night for a different number (the owner of which we knew) and when we explained we were not Albert, the caller might say, "Well, this is Tanguiéta, right? Just go get him!" Things have changed greatly since those days, and now most people have cell phones, just like everyone else in the world.

Traveling was always an adventure, whether it was by motorcycle, car, taxi or bus. Breakdowns were inevitable, so we never traveled without sunscreen, plenty of water, and maybe some food. The amazing thing was, no matter how isolated you seemed to be when you broke down, someone always materialized within minutes, and invariably tried to help—change a tire, or push you out of the mud, or just commiserate and tell you your car was broken down ("No, really?" you thought, as steam billowed out from the engine). Once our car broke down about two hours away from home as we were heading toward the capital. An hour back was the town where our mechanic lived. Not able to halt our southward progress, we just coasted to a stop next to a building, got out our luggage and picked out one of the men who had gathered to watch. Handing him the car keys, Matt asked, "Do you know so and so, the mechanic in N----?" The man nodded. "Would you please get him these keys and let him know the car is here, and ask him to come get it?" The man said yes. A week later, on our way home, as we approached the mechanic's shop by taxi, there was our car. It was fixed, and we drove it home.

Another time we were driving up north and were on a particularly deserted stretch of road with a car that kept overheating. We pulled over yet again and were standing outside the car to wait, when in the distance I saw a walking figure approaching on the road. "It's astonishing," I commented to Matt, "even when you think you are miles from anywhere, there are still people around!" The figure got closer and I saw she had something on her head. "They are so strong! She must be walking for miles with that thing on her head," I observed. We kept watching her. A few moments later, we saw that she was on crutches. "Incredible! Walking so far, carrying a load on her head, and on crutches to boot!" I admired. Next, we saw that she had only one leg! "Impossible! Traveling who knows how long, with something on her head, on crutches and with only one leg!" Almost upon us, we could finally see what her load was—her prosthetic leg! She passed us and continued up the road, and by the time we were back on our way, she had disappeared into the bush.

Some people thought we were crazy for having children in Africa. We had three, and I have to say that I never felt anything but safe there, notwithstanding the machete guys and witch doctors (which were mostly pre-children anyway). If anything, the kids were actually less sick than those of most of my friends in the US. So they might have had a case or two of malaria, but aside from a few colds and intestinal issues, that was it. No ear infections, no strep, no flu, no nothing. In fact, they have been sick far more often in the last four and a half years in the US than they ever were in Benin.

Probably the saddest thing for me was that I never learned any of the local languages beyond being able to greet and get the gist of a conversation, and was never able to *really* talk to most of the women there. I envied their easy companionship with each other—the way they traded babies, did each other's hair, lounged on each other. I always felt like an outsider.

After fifteen years in Benin, we returned to the US. We achieved our goal of leaving the mission in the hands of the Beninese, and also felt a need to return to be near Matt's aging parents, as he is an only child. I love living in Wyoming, and in many ways it was a perfect place to come for the transition back to life in the US. However, my recent experience abroad further changed and marked me, and made me different from most of the people here. I did not realize the extent to which I subconsciously felt like an outsider until I was able to visit Benin again two years later. We were with some friends and I felt so relaxed, so at home. I was with people who completely understood me, and I realized that I never felt this way in Wyoming. I never went through any 'debriefing' either when I moved back to the US at age fourteen, or this time at age forty-six, and never thought about, or verbalized, or even had the vocabulary for, processing the whole range of emotions that go along with repatriating. When I discovered an online community of people like me, it was as if I suddenly realized how I fit into my world. I do miss life in Benin, and would love to live overseas again, but I know we are where we should be at the moment, and now that I'm more at home in my culturally mixed-up skin, I am content.

Middle East

Forbidden Falconing
Chandi Wyant

"We thought about asking you to wear an *abaya* and a *niqab*," Ali says, glancing over his shoulder at me in the backseat. "Because you're not supposed to be in our car."

"Yes. I know," I say.

After a year on my own in Qatar I'm used to the fact that there are very few Western women who've come here solo, and that everywhere I turn I'm confronted by hordes of men.

But this, now, in the Land Cruiser with the two Bedouins, this is more foreign than all of my travels and other expat experiences.

In their culture the only appropriate women in a car with them are their mother, their wife, or their sisters, covered with an *abaya* and a *niqab*.

When Ali had invited me to go falconing, he had said, "It will be you and me and my uncle. Is that okay?"

I had wanted to reply, "Of course. I'm American."

But I knew he'd never met a woman willing to get in a car with men to whom she's not related.

Ali and his uncle don't wear the usual *agal* with the *gutra* loose and flowing. Instead their red-and-white *gutras* are wrapped around their heads, turban style.

"I can't change a tire with it on." Ali had explained to me when I'd asked about the missing *agal*. His reply had surprised me because most Qataris pay the hired help to do a chore like that.

Ali drives quickly, and the Land Cruiser jumps over the bumpy road. The hooded falcon, perched between the seats, seems unperturbed by the jolts.

We go to what Ali calls a farm. "This is where we keep our animals." He gestures toward a goat pen, a camel corral, and a pigeon coop. There is neither a tree nor a patch of dirt or grass in sight. The beige ground is covered with small, sharp rocks.

"We are going to feed the falcon," Ali tells me as his uncle unlatches the pigeon coop and waves us in. "Can you catch one?"

"Sure," I say, though I've never caught a pigeon before. But we had chickens when I was a kid.

The pigeons outwit me at first, leaping and fluttering with surprising speed. I'm determined not to fail in front of these Arab guys.

Ali catches one. I'm narrowing in on a white one, who has gotten herself into a corner.

Voilà! I've got her!

The uncle enthusiastically says something in Arabic to Ali.

I walk out of the coop, holding the soft bird carefully. Her heart beats against the palm of my hand. I stroke her with my thumb, and she looks at me with golden eyes.

The uncle takes Ali's pigeon by the tops of its wings so its body hangs below the long fan of gray wings. I see that to him, the pigeon is simply a thing to feed to his falcon—it is not a thing to stroke. I surrender mine, and it is put with the other one into a plastic cage at the back of the car.

Ali circles the car along various tire tracks, as his uncle directs him, making up his mind as we go about the best place to start the process of feeding the falcon. We park and get out. I follow the guys to the back of the car where the uncle takes out the gray pigeon.

"It's windy, and the pigeon will go too far unless we make it weak." Ali explains to me as his uncle selectively plucks out some of bird's wing and tail feathers. I try not to think of my animal-rights activist friends back in California.

Ali holds the handicapped pigeon while his uncle brings his prized falcon from the car. The falcon remains hooded, perched on the hefty leather glove on the uncle's hand. Then the pigeon is thrown into the sky, and the falcon's hood is removed. The falcon adjusts its eyes for a split second and then is off, streaming through the wind after the pigeon.

Suddenly there's a frenzied rush to the car. "Quick!" Ali calls, and I scramble into the seat that's almost too high to leap into quickly. Ali charges the Land Cruiser across the rocky ground at such a rate that I begin to laugh.

Where's the falcon?

The guys are chattering in Arabic; the uncle scans the sky while Ali rides the Land Cruiser as if it's a thoroughbred released from a starting gate.

"The falcon went this way, right?" he says, glancing back at me.

"Uh, I think so," I respond.

What happens if the falcon doesn't come back? I don't want to ask.

"This is why we bring two pigeons," he explains. "The

next pigeon will bring the falcon in."

We stop and get out. The uncle pulls the feathers off my pigeon's wings and tail.

"The other pigeon was too strong." Ali says.

My white bird of hope is thrown into the sky. Off to the left I see a flash of dark wings. Ali shouts urgently and we leap into the car.

Once again we fly over the rocky ground.

We come upon them; the soft white pigeon pinned under the intense grip of the falcon's claws.

A single spot of blood is on the pigeon's white neck.

Ali turns to me, "The best way to kill an animal is at the throat."

I nod.

"In nature they just know this. If the falcon doesn't kill it quickly, we use the knife. But you see how the falcon has gone for the neck?"

Yes, I see. And I try to push away the memories that surface of my ten-year-old self who, like Emily Dickinson, wanted to help every fainting robin into its nest again.

Just think about the cycle of life, I tell myself. This happens to birds all the time in the natural world.

Ali pulls apart the pigeon while his uncle holds the falcon. Feathers come off, and a piece of meat is held up, attached to a white wing.

Is it the heart? The liver? It is offered to the falcon.

"We can't let him eat too much," Ali says.

The falcon's hood is put back on. The meat attached to the wing is put in the back of the car.

Before we drive away, I notice the pigeon's head, left on the ground. With my shoulders against the open window, my gaze fixes on the severed head with its still-open gold eyes, which had looked into mine, alive, only thirty minutes earlier.

We drive west on the highway. Ali says we're going to 'the tent.' I don't know what this means but I trust him.

We turn off the highway and onto a desert track. A camel and rider, with a baby camel in tow, amble to the side of the track.

"He's taking his camel to breed with the Sheik's camel." Ali explains. "Everyone takes their camels to breed with the Sheik's because of course he's got the best. And he offers the breeding for free."

"That's nice of him," I reply.

"Yes, and then people can get more money for their camels because they've been bred with the Sheik's."

We pull up in front of a large Bedouin tent, made of dark gray goat hair. Nearby is a white tent.

"That's for the women." Ali says, pointing at the white one. "This one is for the men."

"That's confusing." I say. "Because the men wear white and the women wear black."

"Yes." Ali smiles, but he doesn't have an explanation. I wonder why I'm allowed to enter the men's tent. Are these guys breaking a second rule today?

Inside, red-and-white carpets line the floors and the walls. The tent poles are covered in a red material, and red cushions are scattered about. We take off our shoes.

The uncle brings the falcon in and sits on a carpet with his big leather glove on, holding the falcon in the path of the sunlight that streams into the tent's entrance. The brown falcon's feathers have flecks of gold and olive green.

"Do you want to hold him now?" Ali asks me.

"Sure."

I move into the spot where the uncle had been, and I slide my left hand into the glove. Following Ali's instructions, I'm able to get the falcon to climb onto my gloved hand. The uncle hands me the white dove wing with the pale pink meat attached to it. He shows me how to slide it up from below the glove so that the meat is near the falcon's claws.

"Keep your other hand far away!" Ali warns.

I've never been so close to a wild and powerful bird. A grin remains on my face as I follow Ali's instructions and feed the falcon.

After my turn, I sit back and absorb the atmosphere of the tent with its crimson colors, its pesky flies, and the two Arab men. In some other world, someone would think these two men would have certain intentions when they brought me to this tent in the middle of the desert. But I understand that they have no more thought in their heads of touching me than flying to the moon. The concept that it's *haram* to touch a woman to whom you're not married seems to be encased around them like astronauts' space suits.

My mind flashes on the other Qatar I know: the expat culture with the cocktails at glamorous bars in luxury hotels with soaring ceilings, dripping chandeliers, and enormous arrangements of imported flowers. I think of the dancing at Trader Vic's and the jazz brunches at the W.

It's hard to reconcile in my head those places with this Bedouin tent and these two men and their falcon.

I can slip fluidly into the expat scene, but this goat-hair tent and these men in *gutras* and *thobes*, with a falcon needling its beak into raw pigeon flesh, are completely alien to me. Yet, I feel alive here in some kind of lost-world way—as if time doesn't exist.

A quietude comes over my companions when they tuck their legs to one side and lean their bodies onto the cushions. I look at Ali's wide, brown, bare feet, and they seem to say to me that he is as free right now from all the world's ills as he was on the day he was born. These men have dropped into a different energy—as if they have absolutely nothing they must do, as if there is absolutely nothing happening in the entire world.

I listen to their Arabic words and I know the sound of their language will always be tied in my mind with an achingly barren land; barren except for the blood of a golden-eyed bird.

The Price of Beauty
Margaret Ozemet

"I go with you. I translate. It will be fine." My husband could feel my hands trembling. How could something so routine in my country be so terrifying in his?

"How do you know this place is okay?" I asked nervously.

"My mom and sister go there and it is next door, so we try." While location is key for some things, this was not one of those things. "If no good, I find another."

I took one more look into the mirror and nodded in agreement. I was a desperate woman. My roots were showing, my ends were split and no matter how much I wanted to save my salon visit until I returned to a land that shared my native tongue the image staring back at me from the mirror proved that was not an option. I took my husband's hand and followed him next door. Huge silver letters spelling out KUAFFOR CINNAR glared from above the mirrored windows while a little air-conditioning unit dripped on anyone entering. I stroked my ponytail, fearing we soon could be involuntarily separated.

I'd read all about other women facing my same dilemma

as newly arrived expats in Turkey. According to various English-language expat sites, one needed to proceed with caution when choosing a Turkish hair stylist, as the education requirements were shockingly minimal for someone tasked with soaking a scalp in toxins. There were stories of chemical burns, disintegrated eyebrows and the dreaded red. The dreaded red is a Turkish epidemic in which middle-aged women exit salons sporting a shade of red hair generally reserved for clown schools and punk bars. One expat in Ankara had gone to a *kuaffor* in the hopes of returning her grays to her God-given shade of ginger only to exit the salon with hair similar in shade to Superman's cape. She was so traumatized that she hid under a *hijab* until she could return to her homeland for a correction. The horror was palpable.

"You relax. I take care of everything. I tell them what you want. Okay?" My new husband's twitching eyebrow revealed he too was nervous. It was one thing to be responsible for your newly arrived, American wife's survival and well-being in your home country, it was quite another thing to be responsible for her hair. As we approached the entrance, a man was waist deep under the hood of a Fiat, covered in grease. He and my husband exchanged words as Turkish men do, and we walked through the mirrored door.

"Merhaba!" bellowed the buxom blonde with a fabulous head of bouncing blond curls. *"Merhaba"* we replied as we walked in. Her look was totally un-Turkish with the blond hair, muted make-up and chubby bod. She looked far more like one of my people than a Turk, causing a smile of relief to creep across my face. He'd done it. My Turk had found me a good one. I'd learned years ago that you can always trust a chubby hairdresser. Big Blonde continued to chirp

along in Turkish at a clipped pace and I caught about three words of her two-minute monologue. While I stood dumbstruck, my go-to look when trying to translate enough of any conversation to formulate even the shortest reply, my husband jumped in explaining that I was new in town and my Turkish was under development thus he'd be conveying my biddings. *"Tabii!"* Of course, exclaimed Big Blonde as she hugged me like we were long-lost relatives while pushing me into a chair and draping me with a cape covered in evil eyes.

As I scoped out the joint for any signs of beauty carnage, a young woman appeared from behind a curtain painted with even more evil eyes. There seemed to be an inordinate amount of the big blue eyes believed to ward off bad karma in every nook of the salon, causing me to wonder if there was a disproportionate amount of bad juju linked to Kuaffor Cinnar. Before I could question it, the girl from behind the curtain asked, *"Cay veya kahve icar misiniz?"* Finally, something I understood: coffee or tea? I put in my order for a Turkish coffee with two sugars and she was gone like a specter.

With my tiny cup of coffee in hand and bad-juju-protective cape in place, Big Blonde and I began playing an uncomfortable game of look and smile in the mirror before me. What was happening? Was she soaking in the horror that was my hair trying to conceive a game plan? Don't just stand there, girl, get all up in there. Beauty can wait no longer. But no, she didn't so much as touch my head. She smiled. I smiled. She looked away. I looked away. What in the hell was going on? I turned to my Turk busy sipping tea, engrossed in the sports pages in the chair next to mine. "What is she waiting for?" I whispered.

"Cinnar."

"Huh? I thought she was Cinnar?"

"What? No. She is woman. Cinnar is man name." He replied. Damn these Turkish names. But that begged a whole new question, if Big Blonde wasn't Cinnar, then who was?

She smiled at me in the mirror again, then lay a hand on my shoulder and said, *"Burada bekleiz. Az sonra gelecek. Iyi misin?"* Huh? I had no idea what the hell she said so I did what I always did. I just agreed.

"Tamam," I said. By this time I'd been in Turkey for six weeks and *tamam* had become my phrase that paid because it basically meant, 'Okay.' Whenever I was asked anything and a response seemed necessary, I'd found that uttering a simple, '*tamam*,' alleviated all tension and seemed to appease virtually everyone. Unfortunately, I found myself agreeing to some strange situations. For instance, a few weeks prior I thought I'd explained this whole hair thing to my sister-in-law but somehow, after a few '*tamans*,' while I thought we were on our way to the *kuaffor*, we ended up at the mall shopping for swimsuits instead. I didn't need a swimsuit but once you've *tamam*-ed, there is no going back.

While stress sweat began to bubble beneath my evil-eye cape, I awaited Kuaffor Cinnar and pondered what I had *tamam*-ed myself into this time. My Turk had moved from the newspaper to a Turkish soap opera playing on the corner television. How could he be so calm when I was possibly minutes away from receiving the Sinead O'Connor signature do? Sweat was streaming down my cleavage. This was getting real.

Moments later, as promised by Big Blonde, Kuaffor Cinnar entered the salon. I'd hoped for a flaming, Liberace-style Turk clad in a sparkling jumpsuit with a fabulous mustache, I mean, with a title like Kuaffor Cinnar it only seemed fitting. But alas, Kuaffor Cinnar wore a polyester shirt, dark jeans and had the same run-of-the-mill mustache as every other Turk. Ironically, the man I was supposed to entrust with my locks was the same man who'd been tuning up the Fiat out front moments earlier. Lucky for him my hair color would nicely match the motor oil stains under his nails.

There would be no introductions or small-talk, rather Kuaffor Cinnar set right to work pulling a fine-toothed comb through my unnaturally thick hair while clicking his tongue in either disgust, frustration or awe, it was unclear which. He waved an arm to the specter that again appeared from behind the curtain with a steaming cup of tea. While combing and sipping tea he exchanged a few words with my husband as Big Blonde rubbed a glob of motor oil from his chin with a pristine white rag. Not only did Kuaffor Cinnar appear to be a Renaissance man, he was also a master of multi-tasking. I could only hope that quality cut and colors also fell within his skill set.

Amid the flurry of activity, Kuaffor Cinnar spun me around and began slapping a tar-colored paste on my multi-colored roots. God willing he hadn't confused my L'Oréal with axel grease. Within minutes it was over and my head was wrapped in a plastic Kipa bag. As Big Blonde spun me back to home base before the mirror, I heard the door bells tinkle and Kuaffor Cinnar was gone without a word.

For the next sixty minutes I tried to figure out what was happening on the soap opera that had my husband's undivided attention, watched in horror as a woman had her mustache removed hair by hair with thread, and took part in a conversation via charades with Big Blonde. It turned out she was Mrs. Kuaffor Cinnar and had recently had some unexpected triplets, thus her ample bum and constantly leaking boobs. You can learn a lot through charades.

Periodically Kuaffor Cinnar would whisk in and peek under my bag, click his tongue, nod his head and take off again. Eventually, he didn't click and nod but rather whipped off my grocery bag and commanded the girl behind the curtain to rinse me. Silently, the tiny creature led me to the wash station and gave me the wash of a lifetime. Curtain Girl had magical fingers and I was a marshmallow of relaxation for the first time since moving to Turkey six weeks prior. Nothing could harsh my chill... except looking in the mirror.

While my hair was a nice shade of late evening black, free of gray streaks and multi-color roots, I seemed to have developed an unfortunate and rather bold two-inch dripping, black halo stained onto my face. I was so wrapped up in the mystery of Cinnar that I hadn't noticed he put no barrier between my skin and the dye. No cotton, no petroleum jelly, nothing.

"Vat is dis?" my husband had a look of confusion tinged with mild horror. We were scheduled to attend yet another, meet-my-American-wife family dinner that evening and while the black outline would certainly highlight my features, it wasn't quite what either of us was hoping for.

"No problem!" squealed Big Blonde. That was one of the English phrases most Turks learned in primary school and I heard it a lot during my time there. Spoiler alert, it was almost always a problem. Big Blonde first tried soaking her white rag in the lemon-alcohol cologne Turks use for hand sanitizing and hiding BO in the warm months. My halo didn't budge. She tried shampoo and hand soap, but nothing. She called to the girl behind the curtain who brought coffee grounds and while I was exfoliated like never before, the mark of Cinnar remained. Desperate, she held up a finger, the international sign for 'be right back' and left the salon to consult with Cinnar in his station under the hood of the Fiat.

"What the hell is this?" I asked my Turk.

"I do not know. This is not normal?"

"Normal? No! Have you ever seen me with a giant black ring around my face before?"

"I sure he fix it."

Before I could respond the doorbells twinkled and both Mrs. and Kuaffor Cinnar approached with a mild air of panic. Cinnar grabbed the closest ashtray, because in Turkey there is always a close ashtray, and began applying ashes to my halo. I think it's important to add here that I am an Irish American with skin so pale it verges on translucent making the entire issue even more obvious. When the ashes did nothing, he busted out the big guns, straight acetone. Big Blonde soaked her white rag in the bottle pulled from the manicure station and went to work. Finally, after some harsh scrubbing with the highly toxic chemical, the halo lightened enough to be hidden with make-up, but the red flesh-burned highlight remained for two weeks.

With the halo crisis under control, I determined it best to forgo the cut and make a break for it before things got worse. My husband conveyed my desires for a hasty exit to Kuaffor Cinnar who replied hostilely in English, "No!" It appeared that this Turk, like most I've met, didn't believe in quitting. My guess was he needed to find success with my hair because things under the Fiat were not going well. I relented under the condition that no scissors were involved.

Kuaffor Cinnar clapped twice calling his assistants to attention. While my stylist/auto mechanic held the brush,

Big Blonde wielded the blow dryer and curtain girl wiped his sweat while handing him brushes. Why would a stylist need so many brushes for just one head of hair? Because when he was done jerking a clump of hair into submission, he wrapped it tightly through the bristles of a big, round brush and left it there. By the end, my head was filled with about twelve, large, tightly wrapped hair brushes which Big Blonde heated via hair dryer, turning them into old-school hot rollers. While the process was fascinating, I said a silent prayer to the gods of beauty that he knew how to get these things untangled because I knew the kind of damage I'd done to myself with just one brush and let's be honest, he hadn't really demonstrated mastery in the beauty arena.

Left to cool, I was given yet another coffee but between the three hours of processing, the four Turkish coffees, the amount of fluid I'd lost to sweat under my evil-eye cape and the raw acetone that had soaked into my blood supply, I really needed this to be over. When it was determined that I was finally ready for the final wave, Kuaffor Cinnar spun me away from the mirror. I assumed this was to spare me the trauma of seeing giant clumps of hair coming out with the removal of each brush. Well played, Cinnar, since I had no feeling left in my scalp there was no way I would notice hair loss if I couldn't see. And where was my translator and protector through this portion of the event? My Turk paced outside. He had no idea that the pursuit of beauty could take half a day.

As black curls fell to my shoulders I finally exhaled. At least there was still some hair left. Kuaffor Cinnar asked me if I was ready for the big reveal and I nodded, exhausted. With a thickly accented, "Ta-da!" my reflection was revealed. I had hair that was so big it would make a Texas beauty queen turn green with envy. The big, bouncy curls framing my face were exactly what I'd dreamed of—in 1982. I was the brunette yin to Big Blonde's yang. It seemed Kuaffor Cinnar had a signature look and that's exactly what he'd given to me.

It wasn't really a surprise because in Turkey, there was not a lot of individuality in the hair realm. During that time, the majority of the female populous under age sixty wore one of three styles in one of three colors. There was God-given Turkish black, chosen by few, bleached-and-fried-eighties' blond, chosen by nearly everyone under thirty and flaming red reserved for the forty-and-over set. No highlights. No lowlights. No curls. The three styles included the Victoria Beckham inverted bob, the Joan Jet shag or what I'd just received, the Texas beauty queen.

Maybe it was the acetone or maybe it was the heat, but I couldn't help laughing as I tossed my giant hair from side to side. We paid the man and as we walked out the door past the Fiat, I worked the sidewalk like a pageant runway. For the first time since I'd arrived, I didn't look like a foreigner.

We lived in Turkey for three years and in those years I had far bigger cultural traumas than that salon visit—such as an emergency C-section where my husband was mistaken for the surgeon, and an immigration mishap that resulted in my toddler and I being hauled in by the Gendarmes. But just as with Kuaffor Cinnar, we look back and laugh about it now. Within a few months I'd learned to speak Turkish well enough to chat my way though salon visits on my own, though I always made sure to run my vocabulary choices by a bilingual coworker or my Turk beforehand just to be certain. However, even with that I never once left a salon with the style for which I'd hoped. Then again, in a nation where stylists split their time between auto repairs and beauty treatments, what can one really expect?

Returning Home
Michelle Estekantchi

I entered this world with a unique background and often used it in awkward social situations when I fumbled for a topic for discussion. It made me seem much more interesting than I actually felt and usually lifted eyebrows. It made me more memorable. It also provided barriers, created challenges, and gave my life a path that I couldn't help but follow—it comprised my destiny.

I was born in 1978 in Tehran, Iran. Yes, the Iran we all have heard about in the news. At that moment in time, Iran was a hot spot for travelers and expats. It was a very rich country with an amazing nightlife, great skiing, wonderful seaside and large gardens. Iranians had all of the same freedoms that most people enjoy in the Western world today. My mom, a young Canadian girl, moved to Tehran after graduating with a business degree from a university in California and started work as a computer programmer despite having no experience in the field. During her university years she had met some Iranian students who had piqued her interest in the country and, combined with the extravagant expat job opportunities offered by numerous companies, she jumped at the opportunity. She always proclaimed her four years in Iran were the best years of her life. Keep in mind my mother has lived an extraordinary life so the statement is a bold one.

I grew up hearing stories of glamorous surroundings, parties with movie stars and singers, gardens that go on for miles, and a general life of leisure and love. It was a carefree life in a carefree country.

All of that disappeared in 1979 when the revolution changed the face of Iran forever. Like many Iranians, we abandoned our lives there and were forced to begin again in California. I was two years old when we immigrated and never saw the Iran my mom reminisced about. However, the love she had for the country affected my childhood, and I grew up knowing every detail of Iran in its glory days from her constant stories, books, conversations, and movies she insisted I absorb. Perhaps she felt she could replicate the cultural immersion she experienced. She flooded me with love for a country I knew so little about. My dad, a gentle, kind, quiet soul never had that passion for his own country. He was truly Iranian and proud of who he was, but not passionate about instilling patriotism in me. He was always very happy we had an opportunity to move to the United States and always felt there were far better opportunities for us in a country not governed by religion. And that is the introduction to my life and my common icebreaker for awkward conversations.

We remained in the San Francisco Bay area until I was eleven years old. The Bay Area is a diverse, busy, urban, forward-thinking heart of California. At age eleven, I moved back to my mom's hometown in Canada. It was a rural town with a population of approximately 2,000 people. I was the only person who had tan-colored skin for towns, literally towns. My black hair and deep brown eyes stood in contrast to the blond-haired blue-eyed classmates that surrounded me. I remained there for the remainder of junior high and high school. I was both interesting and different and learned to stand with confidence or crumble with my natural insecurities. It was an idyllic place to grow up in many respects. The intimate environment provided me love, safety, security, and a strong education. However, it was not a place rich with opportunities to learn more about my Iranian heritage.

By the time I turned thirty, I graduated with a master's degree in education and worked as a school counselor and private counselor for about eight years on the east coast of Canada. I was promoted to diversity management consultant for a school board and I loved my career. The problem was, I had hit a wall in my career and my personal life. I wasn't married and had no possible candidate. Despite a full social calendar and juggling a few hobbies, I was mostly bored. No matter how full my life was—and it was super full and amazingly great in so many ways—I felt like something was missing, but I couldn't pinpoint what exactly what it was.

In the summer of 2010 during a road trip to Montreal, a friend asked me what I was passionate about and I automatically answered, "Iran."

I always wanted to spend more time there. I wanted my Iranian summer vacations to last longer. I cried endlessly every August when it was time to leave. When my father passed away four years earlier, my passion and longing to stay in Iran intensified, though I never seriously considered staying. I had other goals to follow. But now, in the middle of this road trip's introspective conversation, I realized that Iran was the missing piece in my life. All I wanted to do was to live there. The best memories of my life were in Iran. My large loving family and the best food I had ever tasted were in Iran. Beyond all else, I wanted to live there, the place the rest of the Western world was forbidden to enter.

In February 2011, I requested and was granted unpaid leave at the school board. I will be forever grateful to my supervisor who supported my dream and made it possible. I packed up my nicely furnished one-bedroom apartment and placed all my belongings into storage, save for two suitcases. I began the rounds of good-bye dinners, drinks, and heartfelt conversations. Many people didn't understand why I was leaving. Most just chalked it up to being crazy and reckless. Many cautioned that I was destroying my career and they worried about my financial stability. Perhaps they considered moving to Iran as immature; a gap year way too late in life. Overall, I got a sense that most people were either confused by my decision or felt bad for me in some strange way. However, I had my little crew of people who cheered me on, supported my dreams and understood what fueled my desire to go to Iran. February 14, 2011 was the date that one chapter ended and my Iranian chapter began.

My time in Iran was everything I had imagined. It fulfilled my expectations and then some. The people were extremely friendly. In fact, I decided on my return to Iran that Iranians are the most welcoming people I have ever met. I have traveled to many countries and have never seen people who loved to see foreigners as much as Iranians.

The kindness I encountered, from the people of Iran included simple things like going to a tea party with my aunt and having each lady take a turn to sit by me and welcome me to the country. I watched these older ladies struggle to find words and make sentences just to communicate with me. Even if they didn't speak English they would speak Farsi slowly and endlessly—almost willing me to understand. It was heartwarming. Then there were the more extreme cases of friendliness by total strangers, often happening on a daily basis.

Once I was looking for an English-Farsi dictionary so I popped into the bookstore close to my house. The man was patient with my broken Farsi and once he realized he didn't have the book he tried to give me directions to the closest bookstore that might have one. He could see I was confused so he closed his shop and walked me to the competition! I also got to know the man who sold flowers on the corner from my house. He would give me a flower every morning. He would tell me that he was so happy to see a foreigner in Iran and wanted to make sure I remained happy there. There are endless accounts of the Iranian welcoming spirit I encountered. It made my stay there extremely pleasant.

The family time was soul soothing and the food was delicious. I have nine aunts and uncles on my Dad's side of the family and each have children around my age. They live in a cul-de-sac where all my extended family have houses next to each other and share a beautiful garden. I heard stories of how magical my cousins' childhoods were growing up in that large garden with the friendship of each other to keep them busy. I was always sad I missed out on all that fun. Returning to that garden was magical for me. Spending time drinking tea and listening to my family talk to each other was so calming. They would sit for hours on the large balcony overlooking the garden serving tea, fruit, and sweets. They would chat and laugh and just enjoy each other's company in jasmine-filled air. There are no words to describe how special that memory is to me and how grateful I am that I could share in those moments with them.

The parties were extreme. I was always a girl who liked to enjoy my social life and never shied away from a late night. I have never experienced parties like I experienced in Tehran. I don't feel it's wise for me to write more as I plan to return to Iran. I'll only advise that if you visit this wonderful country, try to make local friends and enjoy the nightlife as much as you can!

My Farsi improved slightly with intensive daily classes and being immersed in the language. There was just so much to enjoy and take in and let soak into your bones. The longer I stayed, the more I considered living there long term. However, I missed the modern conveniences of a developed country. I missed conversing and doing daily things with ease, in English, and I wanted to work again. While in Iran, I had traveled to Dubai for two short trips and loved the city from the time I put my feet on the ground. Dubai ended up being my long-term 'stop' as it provided all of the above and it is very close to Iran so I can visit often and easily.

Looking back on my time in Iran, it's clear that was a monumental time in my life. I feel so lucky that I experienced great joy, learned, laughed, cried, and loved so much. I never could have dreamed of the wonderful life experiences I have had. Sometimes it's difficult to embrace change—like moving to a new country—but when you do it leads to great things. I'm thankful for all those who have been a part of my journey. I'm so lucky to have these people, my family and friends to walk this path with.

The Land of No Logic
Margo Catts

I was warned before I came: Saudi Arabia is the land of no logic. Of course, having that information does little to solve your problem when you're sitting in a guardhouse holding room in the Arabian summer in a polyester robe, sweating profusely and eating weepy tiramisu out of a foil pan because you don't know whether you'll get out before it turns.

Ah, logic. From the Greeks on down, we Westerners sure have loved a well-supported argument. Like, with underwires and suspenders and some full-body Spanx. Of course, the same people who gave us the Pythagorean theorem also gave us a dude who got his dad to throw up all the brothers and sisters Dad had eaten previously, and who then went on to eat his own wife when she was pregnant so that the daughter burst out of his head fully dressed for war... so... maybe we should not take ourselves too seriously.

Clearly, what's logical to me tends to be what I know. Whether it's Zeus and Athena or universal suffrage, making sense of the 'other' can be an overwhelming exercise. When it comes to Saudi Arabia and the Western world, the size of the gap is revealed by the questions I hear most frequently, which generally start with, "Are women allowed to..." or "Do you have to...?"

Ah, er, uh... hold up a sec. Before we talk about driving or dressing or traveling or whatever you *think* you're asking, we need to do a little reframing. The "allowed to/have to" assumes a fixed municipal code, a government of, by, and for the people... blah, blah. And why not? I mean, that's basic, right? Of course, that's not the only assumption underlying the question. The list could go on indefinitely— you assume you're dealing with humans, who breathe air, who address one another vocally... We're leaving *those* assumptions alone, so how are you supposed to know which assumptions *should* be questioned?

Well, you don't. In a new place, all you can do is plunge in and expect to fall flat on your face. Frequently. Say "oops!" and "really?" and "my mistake" on a regular basis. Laugh when everybody else is laughing and you have no idea what you just did that was *so funny*. In Saudi Arabia's case, here's the big stumbling block: public behavior is governed by custom and interpretation more than it is by a fixed legal code. The locals just sort of breathe it in and understand it, but for me it was a matter of acting very conservatively and cautiously until I got the swing of it.

So in answer to, "Do you have to wear..." this is how the *full* answer goes: There is no law requiring women to cover their faces, but conservative Salafist Muslims think they should. So a Saudi woman walking through the mall in central Saudi Arabia with her face uncovered is setting herself up to get scolded by religious police, or taken aside with a demand that she either cover or that a male relative come take her home. Maybe. Depending on the day. And where she falls along an unstated scale of youth and beauty in the eye of a particular officer. None of this will happen to an older woman. How much older? It depends on who's looking. Nor will it happen to a non-Saudi, who may or may not be told to cover her hair, again depending on youth, beauty, hair color, perceived race, body carriage, and again, who's looking. The same religious policing organization behaves more leniently on the coasts, where the prevailing attitudes are different.

Back to the center of the country, inside a restaurant it's fine if a woman chooses to uncover her hair or face while seated, but not once she's up and moving. (In fact, there are all kinds of expectations for sitting that aren't for standing and walking, and vice versa.) There's no actual law that says that the *abaya* (robe) women are required to wear in public be black, but it's just understood that it *should* be. A woman in the mall in a creamy *abaya* that would be considered perfectly modest and downright elegant in Turkey or Jordan is going to get accosted and told she has to leave. Except not on the coasts, again. Or if she's really old. Depending on the officer.

Get it? Of course not. It's a moving target. The biggest clue to how it all works can be found in the proper name of the religious police tasked with enforcing standards for public behavior: The Society for the Promotion of Virtue and Prevention of Vice. Aha! There it is. Whereas Western justice is focused on responding to illegal activity that has already happened, here the intent is to *prevent* bad things from happening in the first place. It's the role of this organization (known locally as the *haia* or *muttawa*) to judge whether a behavior is desirable because it promotes virtue, or undesirable because it might lead to vice.

That uncovered face? It might catch a man's attention

and lead to an illicit affair, which is vice, and must be prevented. Those black robes? They keep individual women from standing out, or their figures from being visible, protecting the women from unwanted attention. This is virtuous, and should be promoted. It spreads out from there. Prayer is virtuous, and should be promoted, so shops and restaurants are required to close during prayer times, five times a day. Candy and red flowers at Valentine's Day have Christian and pagan roots, which are not Islamic, and are therefore vice, and must be prevented. A woman going into a Starbucks that doesn't have a separate entrance for them would be subject to uninvited stares from the men who are there, so we'll shut down that restaurant and deport a bunch of impoverished foreign workers if they allow women to enter at all. You know, to promote virtue. *And* prevent vice. Two for the price of one!

And finally, the kicker. To protect the integrity of marriage and family and home (virtuous), and the actual virtue of women (really virtuous), who are in danger of all kinds of things from licentious men (vice incarnate, all of 'em), women should stay at home unless accompanied by a protective (virtuous) male family member. So no driving, ladies. Note: It is not actually illegal for women to drive in Saudi Arabia. It's *forbidden*. If a woman holding a valid driver's license from another country engages in peaceful protest and drives, there is no driving-related infraction to charge her with. If she's defiant enough, the charge is terrorism. (No lie.) Remember—we're promoting and preventing.

See? The logic is there. You might not like it, but it's there: men can't help themselves and women need to be protected. It's perfectly logical. But the logic starts to get a bit tormented when real life enters the discussion. Saudis used to live in villages where women were surrounded by family members, male guardians were always nearby, everything was accessible by foot, children played freely in the lanes, and chores were done communally. Now city-dwelling Saudis live isolated in their homes, unable to access groceries, household goods, doctors, banks, or schools without a car. So somehow, women *do* need a way to get around during the day when the protective male family member is (presumably) at work. Hmmm.

Enter the hired driver. Problem solved! But—wait. The woman is now in an enclosed vehicle with a male who is not a family member. And she's out in public without a guardian. Eek! But what else are we going to do? *Honestly.* So we'll cook up some justifications that work as long as everybody is agreed that we want them to. Okay, the driver is male but he's foreign, which means he doesn't really count as an actual man. And even though the women are out, which we're supposedly against, they used to be out in the villages, and self-respecting Saudi women are always at least with female friends or relatives, so that kinda takes care of the guardian thing. And arranging for a driver is enough of a pain that they'll avoid going out more than they have to. Give women complete freedom of movement and they could engage in *who knows* what kinds of illicit affairs, even though, it's true, they *could* get to the same places with a hired driver just as easily, so—WHY ARE YOU ASKING ALL THESE PESKY QUESTIONS?

Which is how I ended up in that guardhouse. I had gone to an Italian cooking class with some neighbors from my compound, which is the logical place to live if you want to be able to walk around freely in Western clothes, get your own groceries, and go to the gym. But the class was in a woman's home across town. We couldn't get ourselves there, obviously, and so had to travel in a van driven by some dude who might or might not be a safe driver. (You don't have to go far on Saudi roads to deduce that road safety is not considered a virtue and is not promoted.) Like schoolchildren, we had to be ready to be picked up at a set time, rather than when we were finished and ready to leave. (Maturity, independence, convenience... also not virtues.) So at the end of the class we bolted our focaccia, packed up our tiramisu, put on the robes that would keep us modestly covered outside the compound walls (comfort, not a virtue), and went out into the heat to meet our driver.

The driver wasn't there. Women standing around on public streets making lots of phone calls are assumed to be the worst kinds of women (vice), so the compound guards had to work through a tricky set of competing vices to figure out what to do with us. Streetwalkers at the compound gates? Unaccompanied women in a male workplace? Unsponsored non-residents inside the compound? (Our cooking host was no longer at home, innocently unaware we were having any problems.) Eventually the guards concluded that the lowest-vice option was to relegate us to the no-man's land of the gatehouse break room while we sorted things through.

As it turned out, the driver had gone to the wrong place to pick us up and was waiting there fixedly even though no passengers appeared. (Problem-solving and attention to detail are underappreciated virtues in Saudi Arabia and are not promoted nearly enough.) By the time we got the confusion resolved, however, he could no longer reach us and get us home before having to pick up actual schoolchildren. Other drivers we had in our combined contact lists all had standing school pickup appointments as well, so the final solution was for us to wait for a new driver to be dispatched, who would arrive in another hour. Or more.

And so we waited. Mothers tried to make arrangements for children who would come home from school to locked, empty houses. Someone with an appointment for a medical procedure later that afternoon had to cancel, then make repeated calls trying to find someone who spoke enough English to make a new appointment in the reasonable future. A woman cancelled dinner plans with friends that had depended on her getting home, getting another driver, and meeting them at the restaurant before it closed for prayer. A tired toddler fussed and kicked around the room, bored and hot, while his baby sister cried for her nap. No TV, no music, nothing to read. But at least we had elegant little desserts!

Right about now is when our predicament seemed *just so illogical*. All this distress and upset caused directly by our inability to drive, for the protection of the nation's virtue, when there is *nothing* about the arrangement of using hired drivers that achieves the desired goal. All it actually accomplishes is making ordinary things unnecessarily difficult and hazardous, if not downright impossible. The land of no logic, indeed.

Or at least, not *my* logic. When I arrived in Saudi Arabia, I stepped into the living room of a family I didn't know, with unspoken understandings, expectations, and habits. So much of it seemed bizarre to me. But I'd be a fool to imagine anything different would happen if an outsider were dropped into *my* family's living room. And as time went on, I grew used to the way the reasoning worked, the underlying objectives, the cultural contract and expectations, and I will now jump straight down the throat of anybody who throws the simplistic 'oppression' blanket over a culture about which they know next to nothing. So I waited—overheated and annoyed, but understanding myself to be no one special in a sea of Saudi women waiting for rides, chatting with their cousins and sisters and sisters-in-law, telling themselves how grateful they are that they aren't as unsupported and exploited as females appear to be in my native world.

When other Western women hear me talk about living in Saudi Arabia, they often say, "I could never do that." The absolutism, the wholesale rejection, grates on me every time. I understand that they're comfortable in their own living rooms and those of people who are reasonably like them. But there is nothing to be gained from visiting only homes that look like your own, and much to be lost. We live in a fractured world, full of fear and suspicion and blame, so much of which could be healed if we simply knew each other better. But knowing requires effort. And a healthy splash of humility. There is no way to uncover our own prejudices and properly understand our fellow global inhabitants without engaging with them, living with them, eating their food and exploring their customs and walking their streets. And yes, absorbing their logic. No matter how illogical it may seem.

Asia

A Man from Another Land
Shannon Day

The year was 2002. I was living and teaching English in Osaka, Japan. I had a great little apartment, a few close friends, and the odd date every once in a while. I'd managed to create an interesting array of teaching jobs for myself. Each one took me to a different part of the colorful and cosmopolitan city. I lunched (and practised English conversation) with an art gallery owner. I taught university students, and reluctantly sang songs with preschoolers.

Though I felt restless (as always), I was fairly happy with my life.

And then, one September morning, my dad called from China. He was there, temporarily, filling in for a teacher who was meant to arrive in a few weeks. Unfortunately for the school, she had backed out. My dad wasn't able to stay on any longer, due to other commitments back in Canada. So there I was, being asked if I would come and take the position teaching English and Drama to Chinese teenagers.

But, I really wasn't interested in taking the job.

Jiangmen, where the school was located, is a moderately polluted, industrial city in the south of China. I'd been there once and, in my opinion, it was *not* a destination most Western twenty-somethings would seek out long term. One week there, visiting my dad, had been an interesting cultural experience but I'd been grateful to get back to Osaka, where pedestrian lights told me it was safe to cross, menus had pictures in them, and prospective dates didn't have cages filled with chickens on the back of their bikes.

So, I said, "No, thanks" to the job, and went on with my day.

I taught at the university, met a friend for dinner, and then came back to my apartment where I sat down in the quiet of my own company. And that's when it happened; a sudden rush of panic spread over my body. I was unsure of how or why, but I soon realized that I desperately wanted that job. My heart was racing as I picked up the phone.

A few weeks later, I arrived at the gates of the school in Jiangmen. And, within days, I knew I'd made the right choice. Even the restlessness, I'd consistently carried with me throughout my twenties, seemed to be fading away.

In many ways, life was simple. I lived in a room at the school, as did the other Canadian teachers. They were an eclectic group of people and I enjoyed their company. I also quite liked my students. They were the sweetest kids, so respectful and thoughtful. My routine was far from action-packed and my weekend excitement was found in simple things like taking long, solo walks around the city or sharing a few giant-sized beers and some dumplings on a Friday night with the other teachers.

But, every once in a while, if I felt like sipping a martini, eating Italian food, or mingling with other Westerners, I'd hop on a ferry bound for Hong Kong. The ride was a rocky one but it was well worth the two and a half hours that it took to get there.

On one particular weekend, early in January, I went to Hong Kong to meet a friend who had flown in from Osaka. We shopped and ate and went to see The Big Buddha on Lan Tao Island. We hit the markets on the Saturday night. There we learned that we could hear our fortunes by having our faces 'read.' So, for a bit of fun, I paid the money and sat down to hear my fate. My fortuneteller was a serious looking, older man with thickly rimmed glasses. He simply looked at me, without expression, and then he spoke.

"Soon, you will meet a businessman. He will be from another land." A round-faced woman, his daughter perhaps, translated the old fortuneteller's words.

"You and he will fall in love but you must wait to be together."

I smiled, "Sounds like fun!"

"And then, in time, you will go to his land to live. There you will have a family. There, you will have three children."

"What? Three kids?!" I laughed at the notion.

And that was all he/she said.

While my friend had her reading, I browsed through the handbags and other trinkets.

Then, satisfied with our market purchases and still laughing about what our futures supposedly had in store for us, we hopped in a taxi. Destination: Lan Kwai Fong, a popular bar and restaurant district on Hong Kong Island.

That night, I bumped into a handsome businessman from England and everything else around us became obsolete. I didn't know it yet, but my fortuneteller's predictions would all come true; even the three kids!

Sometimes, when I think about how my husband and I met, I toy with the idea that fate played a hand. Was it fate that filled me with a sense of urgency, as I sat alone in my

Osaka apartment? Perhaps fate, herself, was panicking; knowing that two paths were meant to cross on a January night, in Hong Kong.

But, whether it was fate or coincidence, I'll never know. All I know is, I'm grateful to have chosen the path that led me to a beautiful man from another land.

Coming of Age in the Middle Kingdom
Carissa Cosgrove

It all took place at a time when I thought I understood the world, before I learned that I didn't know a thing. I had missed my connection to Beijing and spent the night at the Chicago airport watching the first episode of *The Amazing Race* and drinking cheap American beer. In the morning I took my transfer early, and made it to my gate with four hours to spare. I couldn't wait to get out of North America—I was ready to start living the life that I had imagined.

I slept most of the flight—I know, it drives people nuts—and woke up as we were making our descent. Hmm, looks smoggy, I thought...

Back in the day there was little English spoken at Beijing International Airport and while I knew my hosts were waiting for me just outside of customs, I had one small problem—my luggage had not appeared on the carousel. I spent the next forty minutes trying to explain to several attendants at the help desk that my luggage had not arrived and I needed it because I had just flown halfway across the world and I wanted my clean underwear and travel guide. No dice. They had no idea what I was talking about. One woman repeatedly asked me; "Do you know Chinese?" to which I repeatedly replied, "*Bu, xie xie*," which was the only Chinese I knew at the time.

Slightly panicked, and wondering if the person assigned to collect me would still be in the arrivals' lounge when I emerged, I decided to abandon my luggage pursuit and embark on my Chinese adventure armed only with my dirty outfit and my wits.

"Have you eaten?" I was asked.

"Not for a while," I said, wondering what sweet and sour chicken balls would taste like in China.

We drove in the near dark for almost an hour, I remember almost nothing aside from the image of a man, probably in his late seventies, face lined and weathered in a way I had only ever seen in *National Geographic*, carrying luggage for a wealthy looking businessman as he waited for his Range Rover escort.

We drove into a gated community lined with homes identical to those you might find in North America, minus the mature trees and extensive properties. We stopped at a house three times the size of my childhood home.

The next morning, which began at 7 a.m., is a bit of a blur. I was shuttled with two other summer school teachers, one whom I had known since childhood, and her delightful Irish beau back to the airport to make our way to Kunming, our destination for this, my first Chinese adventure.

Reacquainted with my luggage, I slept most of the way and woke up just as we were beginning our descent. Seated at the window, I looked down to see green terraced fields and evidence of a city sprawling out in front of me as we hurtled toward the landing strip.

A charming young girl called Cassidy (I didn't know a lot about China or Chinese names, but I was definitely expecting a Lee or a Xing) met us in arrivals and let us know that she would be guiding us throughout our visit.

After our luggage was loaded into a minivan/bus-looking vehicle that would not have been considered roadworthy in North America, we began our terrifying entry into Chinese road travel. We careened through traffic, motorcycles that sputtered smoke and were loaded two metres high with chicken coops passed us on the left, while what looked like thousands of people on bicycles rode on our right. I tried to memorize what I was seeing while I wondered how China managed to progress in this sweaty, coal-burning, chaotic maze of people and animals.

Lunch, which was easily one of the best meals I ever ate in China, and is also one of my top five dining experiences ever, was at the top of a small mountain and specialized in mushrooms which grew rampantly in the high altitudes of the opening to the Himalayan mountain range where we sat.

We ate in a large room with one round table topped with a smaller table that turned so that the dishes, served family-style, were within reach of each guest. We were lavished with what seemed like dozens of dishes, each with its own history and special medicinal and culturally significant properties.

"You will grow strong and makes lots of money if you eat this mushroom."

"These mushrooms grow only during the summer season, you are lucky to be here during such an auspicious time," they told us.

I had already become so lost in the wonder that was

China that I had forgotten why I was really there—to teach English to eager students at a summer school program.

The school grounds were curious. Set just outside of the city surrounded by small, carved patches of agriculture and heavy with the smell of burning coal, the former holiday retreat had been leased to the owners for use as a school. It boasted a six-room building used as the school itself, a large kitchen and cafeteria, an administrative building that also housed the school doctor, a motel-like structure for student accommodations, and several tiny buildings once used for the VIP guests, which would act as our dorms for the next two weeks. We were surrounded by high brick walls, topped with shards of broken glass to deter hobos and thieves, and the gate was guarded twenty-four hours a day by a team of sleepy-but-smiling security guards.

The owners of the past-prime resort had built giant concrete mushrooms around the property, which acted as shaded areas for guests. There were strange representations of Western cartoon characters painted on the walls of each building—recognizable, but off in a way that I can only describe as creepy. How very odd it is to be so enamoured by another culture that we try to replicate it without truly understanding it. There was a painting of an awkward Wile E. Coyote with a butcher knife chasing Road Runner at the door of the cafeteria. I am not an educator by trade, but I can bet that most senior administrators in Canada would have painted over the derelict images before tackling the dangerous teetering thousand-pound mushrooms.

The children arrived. By all accounts, they adored us. I felt famous. They swarmed around us, staring, trying out English phrases, typing Chinese into their translators and surprising us with English words we never knew existed. Eye contact forced them to turn away shyly, but curiosity kept them coming back for more. The two weeks we spent with those children cemented my belief that children are children and people are human, despite our sometimes overwhelming cultural and language differences.

Time passed too quickly and summer camp came to a close. It was time for all students to return to regular classes, me included. I felt, however, that my time in China was not over.

Cassidy, our faithful companion and all-round fun student guide picked me up a few hours early for the airport and took me to a few shops that specialized in teas, dried mushrooms and a multitude of Chinese-style souvenirs for friends and family back home. I had grown fond of the diverse multicultural city during my short visit, and felt that I was not quite finished. When we arrived at the departure terminal, Cassidy thanked me for my time and for my many questions about her city and country, saying she would look forward to meeting me someday when she was in Canada to study.

"I don't think so," I said.

She looked disappointed.

"I believe I will see you sooner than you think," my mind raced with thoughts about how I could get back as soon as possible.

"I will see you soon in Kunming, can we go for bubble tea then?"

She laughed and said that would be great, gave me a hug and off I went into the crumbling building to start my journey home.

Three weeks later, I had packed all of my things and left them in a friend's garage in London, Ontario. I was returning to China to work as an educational assistant for the year. I had abandoned my university education and given almost no thought to the life I was leaving behind, eager only to look again with wonder over those terraced fields as my plane touched down.

It's funny, now as I write this I can think of a million things that would be on my mind should I be repeating this adventure today. I would worry about my parents and family back home, if I could manage tenants in my home from a distance, if the car would still start when I return, if I'd get dysentery or an ugly rash from the pollution, how my son would manage in the new environment, if I would have a social life, how I would get through challenges and if I would stay happy?

During the brief planning of that adventure, one that ended up spanning three years, I barely gave the whole idea a second thought. I decided. I packed. I went. For a whole year. I had about $243 in my bank account and no return ticket.

This time I flew to Hong Kong, and I managed to catch the initial flight and avoid a repeat of my first adventure. I was confident. I could do this. I was terrified. Don't let them see you sweat, I thought. You've got this.

Armed with a prolific set of instructions on how to navigate the HK airport and find my way into the city prepared by my lovely Dad, I headed off in search of my luggage.

I am fortunate to have travelled widely over my lifetime, but I have never seen anything close to the spectacular infrastructure system that makes Hong Kong beat a million times per second. I hopped onto a train destined for Kowloon and stared out my window at the beautiful mess of old, new and nature that makes that city so compelling to me.

That night in Hong Kong was both terrifying and

thrilling. I could barely believe I was there, and everywhere I looked there was a new direction to head in search of further adventure. People were everywhere, cars, lights, sounds, smells—you name it—it took my breath away more than once as I moved about the city pretending I lived there.

I lived in Kunming for one year. I learned much by observing my students and their families, made friends with shopkeepers, learned Chinese, fell in love for the first time, made friends whom I still adore and learned exponentially about myself in the process.

There was a little bar called Golden Crescent in the university district of Kunming owned by a woman named Mae (the trend toward having an English name in China familiar to me by now), it was frequented by expats and I was included.

That part of town was old China, crumbling, stunning, just as you would expect it. Every time you turned a corner in that area, you would come across a wonderful view, sometimes a chicken, and always people and bicycles.

The neighbourhood was being considered as a new location for a police department. Mae and the entrepreneurs in proximity waited to be told by officials to vacate their businesses for the demolition. These people had been running thriving businesses and the government was going to take it away from them? My privileged brain could not believe it was possible.

It was possible; and that stretch of clay, stone and tile buildings was taken down a few months later. The tenants of the shops were given two days' notice on the demolition. We all came out and helped her dismantle the bar. We even climbed to the rooftop and took tiles home—mine was gifted to my friend's father—he found a special place for it in his Canadian garden. To the German who had come to Canada to start a new life after the one he loved had been taken from him—the symbolism of that tile was not lost.

Mae moved to Guilin and opened what became a thriving tourist and expat destination. I visited her there once and found handprints of many of my friends on the wall of her new bar. I am struck now, as I write this, with her fortitude. She built a thriving business, had it taken away, and simply started again—no questions asked. There was a lesson in resiliency I wish I had learned in those years.

Time passed and the school I worked for decided to open a new location on the other side of the country. After my Chinese New Year holiday in Thailand, I would return to a town in Guangdong that no one I knew had heard of. Even my Chinese friends. I reluctantly left my beautiful paradise in the clouds and made my way to the Chinese equivalent of a concrete jungle.

I became depressed in grey, smoggy Guangdong. It is the part of the country that makes the most money and looks least like the rest of China. In 2011, its provincial economy was measured at roughly the same size as that of the Netherlands. It houses Guangzhou—home of the world's largest import-export fair—an event I can assure you will astound any visitor on its sheer magnitude alone. It is the wealthiest province in China, and everyone goes there to make money. I missed my beautiful friends and the music, mountains and sunshine of Kunming.

To ease my frustrations in the new environment, I travelled as often as possible on weekends and without fail on holidays. Weekends in Macau, Hong Kong, Guangzhou, Shenzhen and Zhuhai all had their unique advantages to me. I favoured Hong Kong, and Macau came second—but not a close second, I adored Hong Kong.

Near the end of my third year in China, enter SARS. The virus originated in Guangdong province and the first recorded case was less than fifty kilometres from where I was living. We were given two days' notice and evacuated to Hong Kong. We wore masks sent by a colleague's family. We were quarantined when we arrived in Canada. To me, that was a horrible experience. I never got to say goodbye to friends and loved ones. I returned to China after SARS passed, but I still occasionally grieve for the way I was thrust from a place that I considered a second home.

I travelled many times back and forth between China and Canada, but the time I remember most clearly was a flight from Hong Kong to Vancouver. It was at the end of my first year in China and I was looking forward to seeing friends and family while stocking up on my favourites to bring back 'home' in the fall.

As we flew into Vancouver, which looks quite like Hong Kong—a city tucked into the mountains, I thought about how lucky I was to come from such a safe and plentiful country with all of its rights and freedoms. I was in the middle of my mighty thoughts when the pilot came over the speakers. He said something I will never ever forget, and it is choking me up as I tell you.

He said, "For those of you who are visiting us, we welcome you to Canada. And for those of you who are Canadian, welcome home."

In that moment, and every time I'm reminded of it, I am awash in gratitude to be Canadian. I am forever grateful for my Canadian passport and the privileges that come with it. In some ways, China tamed me; it let me scream out the anger of my youth without consequence. It gave me courage and strength and instilled in me a real understanding of what it means to be 'home.' It let me be me in a formative time of my life and I am certain the lessons would have been very different if I had not packed up and moved to China. *Xie xie*, China.

Stranded on a Non-Deserted Island
Lisa Webb

Everyone knew how I felt about living in France. I shouted my adoration for the country from the top of the Eiffel Tower, and when I got the chance because of an article on my blog, I announced my *amour* for France from the front page of *The Daily Mail*. What wasn't to love about living in a place that was so passionate about the finer things?

In France, life was a postcard. Everyday was a punch in the face of the things dreams are made of. A trip to the market to get groceries was an assault of beauty on the senses. The streets were picturesque, the buildings were stunning, and sometimes the food looked too good to eat. Living in France were five of the best years of my life. I left the country with two irreplaceable, French souvenirs: my daughters. They are baguette-loving, stinky-cheese-eating, little French-girls that can roll their r's like nobody's business and put my six years of studying the language to shame as soon as they utter *le premier mon*.

But staying was not an option for us. My husband may work for a French company, but French, we are not. So when work said it was time to go, we started preparing the boxes.

By ship or by air? That was the question.

We chose air because when the movers came to do the assessment they said we'd have no problem getting the contents of our house into the allotted air shipment space. But of course when moving day arrived the men had finished packing the main floor of the house and let us know that we had four boxes left. They hadn't even been upstairs where our bedrooms were and we were down to four boxes. I called a neighbour, who over the years had become a dear friend and told her to have her husband come over with his company van, the big, blue EDF vans that you see driving around France fixing electrical problems. She was a *nounou* (nanny) who always had a house full of kids, including three daughters of her own. The four EDF truckloads of toys and clothes were much appreciated, and with tearstained cheeks we said goodbye to the French family that had become like our own.

I held my chin high as I accepted the fact that this postcard life I was living in France was over. There would be no more teaching my daughters how to ride their bikes in the driveway of our neighbourhood château. Strolling the cobblestones hand in my hand with my husband on date night with what seemed like a fake backdrop was over. I solemnly acknowledged that there would be no more girls' weekends in Bordeaux and Biarritz, let alone the quick one-hour flight to Rome.

Those days were over. We were moving to Indonesia.

If I thought France to Canada was a long flight to endure with two young children, Indonesia just might put me over the edge. Geographically, we pretty much couldn't get further away from home while staying on planet earth. But, we tried to look on the bright side: there would be amazing beaches, there would be a pool in our neighbourhood, and the weather would be hard to beat. We could do this.

We arrived on the island of Borneo, known for their orangutan-filled jungle, and began settling into a very different way of life. As I stepped outside, still feeling like a tourist, in our non-touristy city, I couldn't help but notice the extreme contrast in scenery to our previous home in France.

We lived in a compound/camp/guarded community, and although we were in an expat bubble of sorts, I still had giant rats in my yard, cockroaches in my living room, ants in my kitchen, and lizards in my toilets.

Traffic in the city was not what I was used to, nor was the litter that lined the streets of the every road. To be honest, it just seemed easier to stay home than to venture out because I found the red-light-optional driving system a cross between terrifying and exhausting.

Our 'camp' had its good points. There was no traffic for one! My daughters' school was just down the street, making it perfectly acceptable to head out of the house for drop-off two minutes before school started. The gym was just as close, and normally completely empty, allowing me to plug my phone right into the sound system and blast my tunes through the entire gym while having a private dance party, if I chose. There was a pool beside the gym that my kids loved and they improved their swimming skills leaps and bounds.

All sounds pretty good, right? So does an all-inclusive vacation resort though. However, take away quality

Internet service, add outrageous long distance plans, a bit of traffic and pollution (on the outskirts of your bubble)—and once you've stayed for a while, the novelty wears off.

What I haven't told you about our compound was that it operated completely in French because of the French company my husband worked for. I'm an all-star in French when I'm in the Anglophone part of Canada where I grew up and no one speaks the language. When I'm in Paris and I'm ordering in restaurants, my language skills shine bright like the North Star compared to all the other tourists. And in the south of France where we lived for four years after our year in Paris, my French skills were good enough to do all the things I needed to do: take my kids to school, talk with the neighbours, visit the doctor... heck I even delivered two babies in French!

But on the other side of the world in Indonesia, I was the sole Anglophone on a compound of thin, well-dressed, cigarette-smoking, espresso-drinking French-women. I was like a piece of Wonder Bread sitting on a delicate tray of croissants. Everyone was nice, but I'm not exactly the Ellen DeGeneres of the party when I'm operating in my second language, unless of course I've had several glasses of wine, which is difficult to do in a Muslim country. So, without the companionship of others who share my mother tongue, I've had a few lonely days on the compound.

When it comes down to it, I am a people-person and I couldn't help longing for my expat friends and the social life that came with them. Sure we spent time with French people in France; many of the other families in our circle of friends were bicultural, having one parent speaking French, and the other English. That mash-up was the perfect balance, as conversations would glide between languages effortlessly. Some friends, and especially colleagues of my husband; spoke only French; as did every single parent at my daughter's school in France. This was a situation that was not unfamiliar to me. I actually learned to enjoy the interactions in French. But I knew that when it came time to relax and really be myself, I had my English-speaking girlfriends who allowed me to let my true personality shine through. I had an outlet to be my carefree, smart, funny self. Something that was a bit harder to do naturally while operating in another language.

Nonetheless, I trudged on as us expats do, working it out however we need to in order to make things work for us, and our families.

I was friendly with everyone and I did have a few girls on camp that were friends. But mostly, I went about my day doing things I enjoyed: exercising, eating and writing. Two of those counterbalanced each other, but at least writing was productive.

Until one day when an expat crisis hit, as it inevitably does at some point along the journey.

We had a driver, which was standard for all expats in our town because navigating the roads and traffic is best done by someone born into the scene. Our driver was a kind man who never lacked for a smile on his face and a willingness to please. One hot and sunny Wednesday morning we were driving the kids to school when he started coughing, as he often did, but I chalked it up to him being quite old and a heavy smoker. As the coughing continued, he actually threw up a bit on his pants, tried to brush it off as nothing, and stifled without success his aggressive cough.

Not wanting to draw attention to the fact that I noticed what had happened, I avoided awkwardness by keeping my eyes forward, a feeble attempt to give him some privacy, and offered a, *"Ca va?"* to check if he was okay. (Yes, even the Indonesian driver spoke French, not English, as he had spent his life bouncing from French family to French family.)

He nodded between coughs, but I was concerned for Pak, as he was quite feeble and although the coughing was somewhat normal, the vomit was not.

When I got home I made two phone calls: first my husband, and then Nadine, an Indonesian/German friend that lived down the street in our compound.

Everyone's train of thought: tuberculosis.

Although practically extinct where we come from, that is not necessarily the case in Indonesia. Before we left we were told the disease was not considered high risk in the country. Since it didn't even exist anymore in the Western world, there wasn't anywhere to get the shot in France or Canada without jumping through hoops to track it down. The travel clinic didn't even offer it. Before we left France my husband contacted other expat colleagues who had already been living in Indonesia for awhile. None of their kids had the shot, so we decided with the information we had, we too would skip this vaccination as they already had a long list of recommended vaccines we were getting as a family and we wanted to avoid the coin sized scar on our daughters' arms if they didn't need it. The fact that our upper arms already resembled pincushions prior to our move to Southeast Asia proved that we were not anti-vaxers, this disease just seemed to be obsolete.

…until it wasn't.

My husband immediately, while still on the phone, e-mailed me links to medical websites on how contagious TB was. If Pak had it, chances are, the kids and I would too since we were always in a closed car with him. It's too hot outside to have the windows down, so if there was a contagious disease in the vehicle, it was all of ours to share. Thinking my husband might be overreacting; I needed to check as locally as I could, without offending my driver. That's when I called Nadine. I told her about the coughing, the vomit, and asked her what she thought I should do. She sprung into action saying she'd make a few calls and get back to me.

Those are the times when it's so wonderful to have a local friend. She was part Indonesian, so she spoke the language and knew the culture, but being also on the expat circuit, she knew my Western concerns. Less than ten minutes later she rang and said that she had called a doctor friend, who strongly suggested we take Pak for a TB test, driving in separate cars. And the moment the doctor thought it was serious enough for us to take separate vehicles was the moment my stomach hit the floor. I quickly slid into a spiral of guilt. We should have tried harder. We should have forced our doctor to find and administer the vaccine. What were we thinking?

As I let my imagination run wild, Nadine took over. She made all the arrangements, picked me up and drove me to the local hospital where we met our driver, who would be tested for tuberculosis. First he visited the doctor, something that was seldom done because of costs. But this trip was on me, I would happily pay for whatever tests and medicines were needed to get to the bottom of this. The doctor listened to his chest and said something in Indonesian.

"They're sending him for a chest X-ray." Nadine translated for me.

I felt sick. That was not the *nothing to worry about* response I was looking for. Images of the pictures of diseased lungs, courtesy of Google, flashed through my mind.

Pak got his X-ray and then we returned to the doctor's office, all executed by Nadine as I spun further into the guilt spiral.

The doctor opened the X-ray, took one look, pointed to a spot on the X-ray and said something in Indonesian. Picking up on my apprehension, Nadine turned to me and quietly translated, "It's positive."

BOOM. Rock bottom on the spiral of guilt was a hard hit. I went pale. My hand unknowingly went to my mouth in shock. I didn't know what to think.

Of course I was worried for Pak, he was quite elderly and we didn't want him to be sick. But I was plagued with remorse thinking of my two young daughters.

I immediately started texting my husband as Nadine tied up the loose ends with the doctor and Pak. She made arrangements for the rest of his tests and explained to Pak exactly what needed to be done, at no cost to him.

"We'll go pick up the girls and get you guys to the clinic." Nadine reassured me, knowing we need to immediately go and get tested.

"Do you want me to roll down the windows?" I said to her joke-serious as we got into the car, not wanting the possible contamination to go any further.

As we drove, with Nadine telling me to stop googling 'TB in young children' I put down my phone and looked over at my new friend with gratitude. I had known her only a few short months, and she took charge in a way you could never expect of someone you've known for such a short time in non-expat life.

And it wasn't just her. Word traveled through camp quickly, and instead of putting our family in temporary quarantine, we were given hands, and helped up when we needed it.

We had to wait three excruciatingly long days to receive our family's TB test results, and I wanted to cry every time my sweet little daughter ran through the house wearing only a diaper. The guilt was too heavy to carry.

"I'm picking you up. We're going to the mall for the morning." Another neighbourhood friend texted me.

"I'm not really feeling up for it." I texted back, wanting to wallow in my misery.

"I'll be there to pick you up in ten minutes. You need to get your mind off it."

I did, she was right.

Another friend immediately offered her driver at our disposal should we need to go anywhere. While a different neighbour gave me the name of a driver she knew that was looking for work.

The women around me stood strong, propping me up, when I wasn't feeling strong enough to do it myself. It's the way of the expat friendship. It is above and beyond any other friendship formed in such short timeframes. For a girl who was feeling isolated by her mother tongue, I suddenly realized that friends surrounded me—no matter what language they spoke.

Our family thankfully was free and clear of TB, and Pak's case was inactive; although since there was conflicting test results on that, we couldn't take any chances. We gave Pak a hearty severance, enough rice to feed his family for the foreseeable future and thanked him for his time with us, although rather short, we truly did enjoy the company of this very kind man.

He taught our family many lessons without even knowing he was doing it. Pak was missing many teeth, which was a bit shocking on our Western eyes the first time he smiled at us. But he wasn't self conscious about that at all. In fact this elderly man had one of the biggest, brightest smile I've seen and he wasn't afraid to use it. It was clear he didn't come from money, but he seemed happier than many financially rich people I've met. He left us with a very human example that money doesn't buy happiness, and my kids, without realizing it, have learned not to judge a book by its cover.

Indonesia is growing on me, just as Paris took a few months to show her charm. I try to not let the traffic bother me, and turn a blind eye to the trash in the streets, for that's not where her strengths lie. I was looking in the wrong places. Her beauty is hidden not only in the beaches, but in the people, with their forever smiles and unfaltering kindness that we can all use as an example.

And as for the expat sisterhood, well, that seems to stand strong no matter where you live, or what language you're operating in. Sometimes you just have to be open to receiving it.

A Celebration of Problems
and Resolutions — A Very
Expat Christmas

Ersatz Expat

In 2012 we were spending Christmas in Astana, the capital of our host country of Kazakhstan. While most of our friends and colleagues used the holiday as an excuse to escape to warmer climes we decided to embrace the cold and ensure that we had a guaranteed "White Christmas" by staying at home for the holidays. In order to ensure that we could still celebrate with family, my mother-in-law flew out to join us.

To set the scene... We went to live in Astana when my husband was appointed the founding Deputy Head Master of Haileybury Astana, a sister school of Haileybury UK, which was, historically, heavily connected with the British East India Company. Kazakhstan is a secular country, but certain Muslim and Christian holidays are dedicated as Bank Holidays so that people get a day off to celebrate.

Most Kazakhstani Christians are Russian Orthodox, however, so December 25 is not a public holiday. There is complete freedom of worship but a ban on proselytising. Astana is also the second coldest capital in the world (only Ulan Bator, the capital of Mongolia is colder); temperatures in December are always below freezing and typically range from -15 to -30° Celsius.

Our home in Astana was airy and spacious, but not particularly cosy. Seven floors up with a double aspect, one side of which faced north, we were exposed to the ferocious Siberian winds. While Kazakh homes are for the most part beautifully warm, a combination of wind and poorly insulated windows meant that ours got very cold indeed. At one stage the internal thermometer was reading 9° Celsius, with the building heating system and no less than three portable heaters running full tilt! The house also had the most amazing lighting system; as our hallway was twelve metres long and ended in a full-length mirror, catwalk lights lined the floor! The rooms were decorated with recessed walls and ceilings lined with moulded polystyrene coving and highlighted with red and green fairy lights. Every room featured a chandelier.

A few days before Christmas Mr. EE had left for a quick trip to the UK to collect his mother for her holiday with us and I was snuggled up on the sofa alone watching a film. The children were asleep in fleece pyjamas under two layers of duvet and I had the portable heaters running full strength. It got to midnight and the electricity went. My neighbours had power and a quick check of my circuit board showed a tripped switch. I turned everything off, set the switch back to normal and then continued without the heaters. The same thing happened again, and again so the system was clearly trying to tell me something. I was the only adult in the house and not wanting the children to wake up to an electrocuted mother I decided to just leave things as they were and go to bed.

Mr. EE plus mother arrived early the next morning, Christmas Eve, and a quick call to work resulted in the magnificently named Soviet, the company electrician, being sent out to help us. A look at the circuit board showed that the lights and electric points for the hallway, two bathrooms, the living room and two bedrooms (including heaters, TV, DVD and washing machine) were all on the one electric ring. A daylight search of the house also showed that there had been a fire in the recessed fairy lights in our son's room. It had put itself out, thank goodness, before it got too bad and certainly our son did not wake nor did the dog notice anything. The thought of what could have happened had the fire got out of hand was just too terrible to contemplate.

Soviet's investigation showed that all the plug points on the electric ring had been compromised and needed replacing, and the faulty lights had to be isolated. A trip to the hardware store was required and I volunteered to drive him. Poor Soviet was a little taken aback, he had expected Mr. EE to drive or for us to pay for a taxi but he took my driving in good spirits. He was, he said, happy to drive if I found it too challenging, particularly given that our car was a stick shift. Women, he claimed, were only able to drive automatics.

For months afterwards I had members of the maintenance and security departments at work come up to me and ask, in hushed tones, if I really could drive our car as well as Soviet claimed!

Before anyone thinks I was driving a Mack truck, it was a small, simple and ancient Nissan 4x4, nothing special in the least. Several colleagues told me later that my example had inspired them to teach their wives to drive their cars. I thought I had struck a blow for women's rights until they confided that it would save them the cost of taxis after a night of drinking—their wife could just come and get them!

A little misogyny aside, Soviet did a fantastic job and our electricity was back in time for us to enjoy Christmas. We had been invited to spend Christmas Eve in the home of some friends. There was no Anglican Church in Astana but an Anglican Vicar from Moscow had visited a few weeks before to hold a service and had left some consecrated host with our friends, which would allow us to celebrate a midnight mass.

Leaving the children with a babysitter, Mr. EE, his mother and I set off for the service. The friend was the Defense Attaché for one of the embassies and we were the only non-diplomat guests. We passed a few black limousines from the Kazakh Security Service on the way to the home. We used to run into them from time to time and they were, without fail, always polite and friendly, Mr. EE was once treated to an impromptu Sunday afternoon of many vodka toasts and sturgeon *shashlik* when our occasional minder decided he wanted to get to know his reasons for being in the country that little bit better.

I dropped the passengers at the gate to the property and parked a short way down the road. As I trudged back through the snowstorm carrying a bottle of wine and food for the potluck—walking through the drifts so that I would not slip over—I was put in mind of the carol of Good King Wenceslas. Even with all the heavy outdoor clothes it was a relief to get into the warm and dry, the last person to arrive.

The service was both comforting and familiar and strange and unusual. I had never been to a communion celebrated by a layperson before and the forms were not quite the same, but the meaning and the faith behind them were exactly the same as would be found in any church on Christmas Eve. That little celebration was the perfect microcosm of expat life as we broke bread with Americans, South Africans, Germans, Brits and others. After the service we shared Christmas delicacies from our home countries and spoke of the traditions that are dear to our hearts.

Everyone (with the exception of me and a few other designated drivers) enjoyed the mulled wine and hot cider; some rather more than others. Mr. EE was cornered by a garrulous German man that we had not met before. Everyone there was, he declared, a diplomat or government employee of some sort and he was convinced Mr. EE was as well. "You can tell me," he said in a staged whisper, "MI6?" It made us smile and he just could not be dissuaded, particularly given the School's long heritage with the UK Foreign Office and the pundits of the Great Game.

My mother-in-law who had arrived only that morning had debated whether or not she should come, not certain that she would be welcome and it took us some time to convince her she would not be out of place. Of course, as is normal with expat communities around the world she was immediately welcomed as 'one of our own' a member, no matter how transient, of the expat tribe of Astana. The evening was the first time she truly understood why we chose to live this expat life and the benefits it brings to us as a family.

As I trudged, Wenceslas-like, back through the snow to heat the engine enough to move the car to the gate I saw some activity in the darkness a way back and as we drove away a dark car peeled off and followed us home. No doubt they were grateful that their shift was at an end. Knowing that it was our Christmas Eve, the security guard for our building came up to us as we parked to congratulate us on the holiday.

The fun did not stop there. A few days after Christmas I drove to the airport to collect some friends returning to Astana after maternity leave. The idea was that I would drive the mother, baby and grandmother who was coming to help out for a few days and the father would go in a separate taxi together with the luggage. We managed to get everyone into the two cars and to the house only to find out that the landlady who was supposed to be there to let them in had not arrived. It was four in the morning and the taxi driver was getting restless so with no other options and needing to get the tiny baby into the warm we had to go back to our house. We pulled out the sofas (the house had three sofa beds, thank goodness) and manhandled the 10 suitcases and travel cot into our hallway. The family were able to grab a few hours' sleep before the landlady turned up. Unable to find a taxi, the family, Mr. EE and I had to ferry everything over to their home in the one car but the landlady was fantastic. She was so upset to have missed the pickup that she welcomed the family with homemade jams and cooked a *beshbarmak*, a traditional Kazakh dish for us all to share.

As always with expat life, what goes around comes around. Just after New Year Mr. EE spent the weekend travelling to the UK on a quick turnaround to take his mother back home. I was sat, curled up on the sofa watching the sequel to the film I had been watching when the switches tripped. Close to midnight our daughter ran into the living room to tell me that her brother was not breathing. Running to see I found him in the hallway, his lips turning blue and struggling to breathe. He was still getting some air and he seemed to calm down and ease his breathing a little when he saw me. I thought it might be an epiglottis but wanted a doctor to check it out. Sitting in a bathroom with the hot water on full I called the insurance emergency line. To our horror, they refused to send a doctor out (our bells-and-whistles insurance was apparently not quite what we had been promised, something which the company remedied shortly after this event), but told me he sounded bad and had to go to the children's hospital A&E. They were able to give me the address, but when I tried to call the emergency translator I could not get through to her mobile. I was in a complete bind, at home alone without someone to look after my daughter and I did not relish the thought of dragging two young children through the cold dark night. In desperation and just to hear a friendly voice I called my friends and a few minutes later there was a knock on the door, the father of the family we had collected from the airport ran over to our home to sit with our daughter. I bundled our son up as warmly as possible so that the cold air would not make his condition worse and off we set to find the hospital.

While I had the address I had never been to the hospital before and I spent some time driving around the streets trying to find it until I ran into a road police patrol. Not typically noted for their friendliness they took pity on me and gave me directions. Once we arrived at the hospital things got really strange.

The hospital was completely deserted; it looked like a set from *The Shining*, broad corridors completely empty and echoing with my footsteps. I searched the signs for any mention of 'emergency' or 'A&E' but found nothing. I even took a chance and shouted out a cheery hello in Russian but received no response. I called the insurance again but they had recently had a shift change and were less than helpful, I tried my emergency translator's number again with still no luck. Our son, who had been getting better at home, was now going blue again and struggling to breathe. By now my Kazakh phone had run out of credit and I was using my emergency UK-contract mobile to make calls at frightening expense. Mr. EE, back in the UK, was also trying to get hold of the insurance co-ordinator and the translator but with an equal lack of luck. I was just debating driving to a public hospital that I knew had A&E or whether to go home and try to manage things there until morning when a nurse walked past. She directed me to the out-of-hours medical cover; it was unmarked, through a tiny door at the back of the hospital and they had been waiting for me. A short call from the insurance to their main line would have told them I was in the building and looking for them.

The duty doctor was very efficient and friendly, sorted out a nebuliser for us and gave us some medicine. It was not an epiglottis, thank goodness, but a rather nasty bout of laryngitis. Apparently the symptoms he presented with would have generally required our son to go to the isolation ward at the public hospital but as he was a borderline case, she was happy for us to stay at home unless his fever rose to a certain level. As we were without a translator she was very kind and spoke as simply as possible. She also ran her prescription and instructions through Google Translate to make sure that I understood them accurately.

On a stressful night it was an absolute godsend to have friends on whom we could rely. The friendly father had a hot drink ready for me when I got home and helped me put the children to bed. He and his wife even stopped by the next day to make sure that we were all okay.

The feeling of welcome and community that we felt on that unusual Christmas Eve was not an illusion, it was there for me when I needed it most a few weeks later as it has been in almost every posting I have lived in. It is, and always has been, one of the best aspects of expat life for me.

Colours That Do Not Exist
Marcey Heschel

In February we hired Divina. She's a twenty-five-year-old Filipina who lives with us, cooks for us, cleans for us and helps us care for Sophia. One of the 'extravagancies' per se of living abroad in Southeast Asia is the affordability of hired help. I consistently hear comments from people at home about how lucky we are to live here and have help. People say, "Oh, must be nice to have a maid," or "Get the maid to do it." We don't call Divina our maid. She's our helper. It's a more polite term. And although we appreciate the help to the utmost degree, we don't just "Get the maid to do it." We respect Divina as an individual and as any employer should respect any employee. In fact, having help did not come naturally to us.

Greg and I have struggled with such stratified socio-economic differences, and the fact that somehow in this dysfunctional and unfair world there are those who can hire help, and those who are the help. Instead of this being a server-servant relationship, we look at it more like Divina is helping us immensely and we too are able to help her by providing a nice home, healthy food, a good salary, a safe working environment and hopefully a family that makes her separation from her own a little easier.

I must say that the ability to sleep in till 9 a.m. on a morning following a long night with Sophia does however feel like a luxury. Nonetheless, having Divina with us through my three months of pregnancy sickness felt necessary and not so luxurious. I threw up every day multiple times. Divina was there to help with Sophia and make me noodles when I could eat them. Divina makes the best noodles. She was there through my miscarriage and D&C last April and she has become my friend and a part of our family. In fact, I don't know how I would have gotten through those times without her. I taught her my Western recipes and she picked them up easily. She's a skilful and careful cook and she prepares all of our personal dishes now, although I dare say she cooks them better than I do... even banana loaf. Working for an Indian family before us, I was surprised she was able to switch from curry and roti to roast chicken, potatoes and gravy without a hitch.

Divina's story is probably not an unusual one. It is probably more common that I'd like to imagine and with her permission I would like to share it to juxtapose with our first-world problems.

Divina is twenty-five, as I mentioned. She became the mother of Charles Justin and Queen Jasmine before she turned eighteen. Being a young mother in the Philippines brings its challenges but for Divina those challenges were com-pounded with her children's father having a debilitating eye condition resulting from Marfan's syndrome, which has left him unable to work.

Divina's factory job, making hard disc drives and medical syringes, earned her approximately 13,000 Philippine pesos a month, the equivalent of about US $278.

Between expenses for electricity, drinking water, rice and groceries they were unable to save anything and felt desperate. With two young children and a non-working partner, Divina had to make the only possible decision made by thousands of Filipino women a year. With a heavy heart but a commitment to providing for her family, Divina boarded a plane bound for Malaysia in hopes of becoming not only the reproductive, but also the productive force of her family. She left her four-year-old daughter, five-year-old son and the father of her children behind. She was twenty-three at the time and was encouraged to join her mother-in-law in Kuala Lumpur. She was devastatingly sad to leave but nothing about it seemed alien, as so many women she knew had had to make a similar choice.

In many ways, the Philippine economy relies on the money these women make and send back to keep the economy afloat. The remittances of overseas Filipino workers far surpass foreign direct investment in the country. Yearly remittances calculate to about US $12-14 billion, which doesn't account for the thousands of illegal workers who also send earnings back home.

Divina spent approximately eight months at her first placement with an Indian expatriate family. She was one of two cooks and learned quickly how to live with a family and become a domestic helper. She prepared all meals and took care of a seven and eight year old before and after International school. The great paradox of the situation for these Filipino women is that they leave their own domestic life and children to care for someone else's.

The wages earned for a domestic helper in a country like Malaysia are over double that of a single factory wage in the Philippines. The conditions in those factories can be precarious at best, but the situations encountered in foreign homes can also be chancy. Some of these labor migrants are mistreated, abused, or sexually harassed by employers. Many have had their wages withheld and have encountered unspeakable cruelty. Divina fortunately has not experienced any of these calamities, and therefore she still has an incredibly positive outlook on being a domestic helper. We are fortunate to have someone so young and virtually untouched by these hardships.

Upon Divina's first family being transferred back to India, we were fortunate to hear of her availability. We interviewed her and she has been with us since February. It wasn't long before Divina and I became close and she felt comfortable enough to share her story with me. Her eyes light up as she speaks of Queen Jasmine and Charles Justin, but there is a certain sadness there that a mother should never have to bear. Being a young mother myself, the thought of being away from Sophia for any reason whatsoever is heartbreaking to even ponder. I cannot imagine the courage it took a young twenty-three year old to take full responsibility for her family and leave them in hopes of providing for them more adequately. Prior to this summer, Divina had not seen her children for nearly two years.

There are times in our condo where Sophia and I listen to our special mommy-daughter songs and dance the afternoon away. On more than one occasion, I have glanced over to the kitchen only to see Divina's eyes full of tears. Sometimes her pain is overwhelming. She has told me that the loving music makes her want to sing and dance with her own children. I hug Divina, Sophia hugs Divina, but we cannot possibly fill that void.

We took Divina to the water park this summer. She was over the moon about it. She had never been to such a place and when we asked her if she would join us she couldn't control her excitement. She and I rode the most massive funnel slide and she screamed, "Unforgettable, Miss Marcey!" and I knew she truly meant it. Experiencing such simple joy is humbling for us. When something small can mean so much to someone, it can fill your heart to take part in that with him or her.

Part of our arrangement with Divina is a trip home to the Philippines each year. This is quite customary, and so we sent her back in August. The emotion involved in finally seeing her children and wrapping her arms around them was beyond measure for her but she told me all about the tears her daughter shed when Divina would leave her classroom. The separation anxiety exhibited was intense, and having their mother home for such a short time was almost like opening a wound. For Divina, it sent her into an internal battle of wondering just how she could move back to the Philippines because leaving again would be unbearable. She did nonetheless return to us because, she said, she'd made me a promise but also because she knew she had no fathomable choice. The day before she left, she was able to legally marry her children's father and that provided her with a sense of happiness to tuck into her self-sacrificing suitcase of responsibility.

Divina and I have spoken a great deal about her situation and I find it perplexing because usually to most problems that I have encountered, a solution can be conjured up. This is not the case for many people in our world. For Divina, it seems sometimes like the only solution is to find a sense of fulfillment and happiness in the existing situation, but Skype and Viber cannot hold her crying children when they are sick.

Although moving back and being with her husband and

children would be the one answer to her prayers, she knows she couldn't provide any more now than when she left. Her husband's eye condition leaves him unable to work and a one-income factory salary could simply not support them. The only solution would be for her husband to get the surgery he needs on his eye. If that were possible then likely six months after that he could also find a factory job. If both of them could obtain employment in the Philippines then they could live together as a family and have just enough to pay for the electricity, as well as buy rice and drinking water. Together they might be able to bring in about US $600 per month. Without any education neither of them could hope for more without one of them moving away again.

The situation with employment in the Philippines is unworkable. Over the years promises of job availability have been made but most growth in the Philippines has been jobless.

The labor remittances from women like Divina help keep the economy afloat.

Divina's home in the Philippines is less than 200 square feet. They have a pump that provides dish, laundry and bath water, but they have no shower. The house has many leaks and they are consistently dealing with these troubles during monsoon season. They manually flush the toilet with a bucket of water, but at least they have a toilet. The circumstances are difficult to imagine in many ways, but all Divina could ever pray for would be to be with her family, in that house and all snuggled up together in bed as they were in August. Nothing else really matters but being with the ones you love. My heart aches for Divina some days, and when I'm feeling down she can lift me up just by being in her presence and remembering what she's doing for her family and how humbling that is.

We are working with Divina on a savings plan that will help her reach her financial goal, but it will take years for her to make enough to send home as well as save for her husband's surgery. We will continue to help her in any way that we can.

I feel fortunate tonight to climb into bed and snuggle our little Sophia. But I say a prayer for Divina's children, husband, and all the women who have to selflessly leave their children in order to do a mother's duty and provide for the ones she loves more than anything on earth, including herself. Tonight Divina's T-shirt reads, "I dream of you in colours that do not exist." She sends her love back home.

A Year of Magic, Mystery and Chaos

Gabrielle Yetter

It's no longer stinky. It's aromatic.

The broken-up sidewalks and chaotic traffic are not an irritation. They're an amusement.

Even the searing heat and torrential rain are no longer intolerable. They are just vehicles for bonding with neighbors and friends as we sweat, mop our brows and laugh at one another.

Things change.

When I first arrived in Cambodia, I didn't think they would. I'd come to Phnom Penh with my husband, Skip, to put down roots; to volunteer and start a new life in a country we'd never visited before.

I was excited. Thrilled at the prospect of experiencing life in a gentler part of the world and energized at the idea of breaking away from the norm.

But it wasn't what I expected.

I thought it would be more sophisticated. I expected quaintness and charm. And I was sure I'd fall in love as soon as I arrived.

I didn't think I'd be confronted by dirt, ugliness and squalor five minutes after leaving the airport. Rats outside our guesthouse, unpleasant smells on every corner, blocked drains, sweaty, dirty skin from dawn to dusk. And the feeling we may have made a horrible mistake.

I didn't fall in love. In fact, I wanted to cry and hide myself from the blazing sun and smelly streets in an air-conditioned hotel room and watch TV all day. This was our new home. I was miserable, disappointed and hot.

But things changed.

Contrary to the idiom '*familiarity breeds contempt*', in my case it was the opposite. Familiarity brought insight, compassion and love.

Within a couple of weeks, I didn't notice the dirt—I saw a tiny, brown-eyed girl playing with a puppy in the sand. Within a month, I didn't recoil at the sight of bloody slabs of meat hanging in the market—I watched street vendors barbecue them and serve them over spicy noodles. And before long, I didn't whinc about the stifling heat—I jumped onto the back of a moto or headed for an air-conditioned coffee shop.

And, a year after arriving, I found myself defending Cambodia and its people more staunchly than I defended my own homeland.

I'm not sure when I started to fall in love. It may have been once we moved into a place of our own or when I started work at an NGO and had a regular place to go every day.

I do know, however, that I started to avoid many of those expat coffee shops and restaurants I initially craved. I found myself drawn to places where I mingled with local Cambodians, complete with dirt floors, dogs under the tables, bugs flying around badly-wired ceiling fans and dishes such as *pigs arm of maple*.

Don't get me wrong. Cambodia is far from Nirvana. The government is corrupt, the history is gruesome, there are no social services or decent healthcare and people starve, become terminally ill and get evicted from homes they have lived in for twenty years.

But, for me, the country has an irresistible charm that shows up in its gentle, childlike people with their quirky customs, constant smiles and delightful sense of playfulness.

Driving to work in a *tuktuk* every morning, starting my day with a heartwarming hug where children, street vendors and moto riders smiled and waved. And misspelled signs such as '*Sour Wedding Embellishment*', '*Hair Falling Down Shampoo*' and '*Crap in Curry Sauce*' made me laugh.

I've eaten snake and roasted crickets, ridden a five-hour bus journey on a plastic stool and pushed a *tuktuk* up a hill. I've gotten lost jogging through a Muslim village, hiked up Phnom Bakheng at dawn to watch the sun rise over Angkor Wat and learned how to speak a language I'd never heard of.

I've dusted bugs from my breakfast cereal, watched a rat run across our living room floor, boiled water for drinking and toasted slices of bread over our gas stove before we broke down and finally bought a toaster.

I've interviewed indigenous women on remote mining sites, listened to stories from colleagues whose families were murdered by the Khmer Rouge and helped raise funds for our *tuktuk* driver friend to build his first house.

I've heard sirens scream outside our windows on the hideous night when the Water Festival stampede claimed more than 450 young lives. And I've knelt in pagodas, bringing offerings of money and food on the holy days to remember the dead.

I've also eaten freshly shucked oysters and sipped margaritas on beaches as the sun set over the Gulf of Thailand. I've heard world-class jazz in a Phnom Penh cocktail lounge and savored cupcakes better than any I've ever tasted. I've awoken to the sounds of the jungle from a room open to the elements and I've travelled to other regions of Asia on airline tickets costing only a little more than a dollar.

Far from my original fears of not being able to find anything, I've found everything.

We've also found we learn valuable lessons from people who earn $2 a day.

We've seen how people with no money can be filled with integrity and gentleness. And that a country with a devastating past can forgive, move on and live a true Buddhist existence.

While we have spent the past months living, learning, meeting, talking, watching and experiencing, I have a feeling that, even years from now, we will still be clueless about the real way of life in Cambodia.

But one thing I know for sure. I'll know when it's time to leave. It's the day when we walk down the street and smile at these gentle people. And nobody smiles back.

The Dawn
Kimberly Tremblay

I had been struggling making new friends, finding a new routine for my two-year-old daughter, four-month-old son and myself. I considered myself an introvert with an extroverted streak, if that makes any sense, and thought when I moved to Malaysia from Canada that I would find a handful of good friends shortly after moving to my new place. Well, it was now month three and no friends.

It wasn't that I hadn't been trying. I smiled. I laughed. I made eye contact with everyone and anyone. And I mean anyone. Grocery store clerks, random people on the street, other parents at my daughter's school—no one was biting. I felt lost and alone. My son, being very young, also made getting out more difficult. I was breastfeeding in a foreign Muslim country, which terrified me into hiding in back rooms so I wouldn't offend anyone (I later realized this was my misunderstanding). And I was stuck to his schedule of napping at home, which confined me to our empty apartment. The lack of sleep probably didn't help my feelings of rejection either. I would see gaggles of women with children at the playground and I would smile or try to strike up conversation and it would go nowhere. They would smile back; ask a few usual questions and then move on. It was hard.

My husband would try to reassure me that it would get easier once our son was older. I felt desperate for companionship in a way I never had before. I felt something was wrong with me.

A few more weeks passed and my daughter developed an abscess in her gum line from a fractured tooth from before we left Canada. We brought her to the 'best' hospital we knew of. Navigating a new medical situation with a new-to-me dentist was difficult, so we decided to consult our previous dentist who had seen the X-rays and who we trusted. He informed us the baby tooth had to be removed. The dentist in our new country thought that it could be salvaged. With two very different perspectives, we decided to trust our previous dentist and have the tooth extracted... our two year old was going to be sedated and have her tooth pulled.

The next week, my husband was restraining my daughter while she screamed and squirmed in the dentist's reclined chair. The anesthesiologist inserted a large needle into her hand and the dentist pulled the tooth from her small mouth. Screaming, blood, and panic were the best three words to describe our situation.

However, my daughter was at the playground the very next day. She was happy and forgot all about the pain from the day before. And that's when I met her. Dawn. She came over with her cheerful smile and three children running about. She said that she has seen me around and wanted to bring me to a few mommy functions in the area including a coffee meet-up the next day. Wow, I suddenly had a social calendar. I was so excited!

Dawn brought me to a local coffee spot and we met up with another new mom in town. We had lattes while the kids moved tables, played boisterously and made messes. It was fantastic and everything I needed after a long couple months of limited conversation and stressful events.

From that point on, I realized I needed to be more aggressive in my friendship making. While I was at the doctor's office with my son I noticed another woman with a child around the same age. I struck up a pretty basic and somewhat lame conversation, "How old is your child," "Where are you from," "Where do you live," "What's your name," etc., which I guess probably looked like a barrage of questions fired at a poor bystander. But she took the bait and left me her name, Claire, and number with the nurse so we could have a play date together sometime. I was awfully proud of myself and thrilled to have another friend added to my repertoire.

Less than a year later, Dawn and Claire are now both leaving the city. Dawn and I never became very close, but the people she connected me to became like family. When Dawn approached me to invite me out for a simple coffee, I felt my life change. Claire and I spent more time together, as our children were of similar age, and I felt like I could handle living in a foreign country and starting anew. I will be forever thankful for both of their friendships and their willingness to take on a new friend.

And thus continues the cycle of friendship for expats. People are constantly coming and going. It ebbs and flows throughout your stay, pushing you from the new kid on the block to experienced resident in a matter of months. I have internalized the aloneness to a degree that frightens me should another post become an option. I want new people to feel better than I did, so I completely turn off my introverted side when I see a new face. I start the barrage of questioning again, this time as the experienced resident. The "Where are you from," "Where have you been," "How long will you be here," etc., opens the door to new friends for me and hopefully allows the newcomers to feel a sense of connectedness. And even though I may never become close friends with every new person I meet, I hope through our conversation, they feel a sense of belonging. It may be me that connects them to other people they grow close friendships with, ending a bit of the solitary struggle I felt in my early days.

Feels Like Home
Nicole Webb

Tears! Prickling at the corners of my eyes, threatening to make an unruly splash into my freshly made cup of coffee (thanks, Dad). I hastily swipe them away, in the hope no one can see that I'm 'welling up'... over a television commercial!

Who cries at the telly? Is it just me or the older we get, do we get more emotional, more aware of the fragility of life? Of course being a mother doesn't help... and yes, I'm just going to say it, nor does... being an expat.

So, what had this usually hardy expat feeling like a sentimental old fool in her mum and dad's lounge, in the great land down under? It was an advert by the flying kangaroo of all things. Yes, Qantas. Flying and airports... how convenient! The one thing we expats are all too familiar with.

No matter how many times I watch it, it never fails to produce a chorus of emotions within me... I mean it's made for people like me. Expats. Expats living in faraway places, far removed from the comforts of home; expats for whom hanging in an airport lounge probably happens more regularly than hanging in your mum and dad's backyard and goodbyes, well, we all know how painfully regular and perpetually difficult they continue to be (no matter how long you've been doing them)!

The ad is called "Feels Like Home" and is a series telling the stories of five people who've been living overseas, away from home. It shows them in airports and on flights heading back home, into the arms of welcoming loved ones: emotional grandparents seeing their granddaughter for the first time... and saying goodbye to her. Can it get any more heart-wrenching! The song itself is enough to push me over the edge.

So, as an expat who's just flown in from China, halfway around the world to be tucked safely on her parent's couch, Tim Tam 'choccy' biscuits in hand and good old Aussie TV blaring away in a language that resonates... Qantas you got me!

Fast forward three months and I'm back in the city of Xi'an, in far-northwestern China—where I'm currently residing with my hotelier husband and five-year-old blondie, on our second expat posting. It's a day when it probably looks and feels like anything but 'home'.

After all I am an Aussie girl, there's not a Tim Tam in sight and it's snowing! Little flakes of white are fluttering their way to the ground, swirling around me in a strange but delicious fashion. My British husband laughs when I tell him, looking out of the windows that I feel like I'm trapped in a snow globe. Definitely not a seasoned winter wanderer, I spent the first winter here wrapped up as tight as a sausage in a hotdog bun... constantly grappling with what to wear in minus temperatures and how to keep warm from head to toe and then cool off inside when the heaters are on high and I break out in a sweat in my sixteen layers.

This winter though, I'm getting the hang of this frozen thing. Okay, so I'm not quite Elsa, but I do find myself frolicking in the white stuff, sans scarf and thermals with all the enthusiasm of Olaf. Who is this girl looking back at me in the mirror, in a puffer jacket!?

Having been on the expat roundabout for about five and a half years now, I'm a firm believer that there comes a poignant moment in your adopted place of abode where it suddenly feels like home or at the very least your 'new normal'... as normal as living in a city where few people speak your language and you're the only blonde within a ten-kilometre radius. It's akin to letting out a gigantic sigh of relief; the coil that's been wound tightly seems to unravel with an unexpected lurch.

For me, it's usually around the nine-month mark... (and almost as unpredictable and bumpy as a pregnancy). The penny drops or something drops (hopefully not your baggy thermal underwear).

For a brief moment—hopefully a little longer—you feel like you're where you're supposed to be. You're not the stranger in a foreign land; the onlooker observing an alien world; the weird white woman skulking through town hoping no one will notice her—the object of much staring and speculation.

You are part of it! Loudly and proudly. Suddenly you feel like a legitimate community player, who can line up and order a damn coffee with the best of them.

Ironically, my penny dropped one sunny pollution-free morning, when I tried to order a coffee, no cream, skim milk in Chinese and the cashier (to my fist-pumping delight) told me what great Chinese I had. As someone who's at the stage of having to repeat what she's going to say over and over, for a good ten minutes before entering the store—usually only to be giggled at and left standing mid-sentence while they run off to find the most fluent English speaker in the room... I could've hugged him right there and then.

It began what was a month of many firsts in my 'new normal'.

For starters, the regular adrenaline-fuelled school run became bearable. Usually a blood-pressure-raising journey across town, for months I had endured it with my eyes squeezed tightly shut, fingernails digging into the leather seats and stomach doing little flip flops as we roared through peak-hour traffic on the wrong side of the road (for me anyway), cars criss-crossing in all directions, weaving in and out of their lanes, mere inches from my face.

The ear-splitting sound made by the myriad of horns screeching from every direction had, without warning, become a dull roar in the background. Nothing to be phased by.

I found myself unexpectedly kicking back (a little too calmly if you ask me) heart rate at an acceptable level, an amused smile on my face as I watched 'China life' pass me by in all her glory; utterly oblivious to the fact that cars were almost on top of us and we'd had thirty-three near misses!

The sight of old rusty trikes rattling on by, loaded up with precariously balanced goods, not to mention people— all competing for a small piece of the road, among overcrowded buses and unperturbed taxis—was hardly even photo-worthy. Not so much as an eye boggle in sight!

Scooters and motorbikes slid in and out of morning traffic, often with three or four people squished onto the seat, kids sandwiched in the middle, all helmet-less. The ubiquitous cigarette dangles from many a rider's pursed lips. (I'm no longer wasting precious time worrying it's going to fall out.)

I can't remember if it's strange to see a woman sitting sidesaddle on a motorbike in high heels, talking on her mobile? Is it normal to see cleaners in their bright 'orange is the new black' uniforms, dotting every street corner, massive brooms made from long, spindly twigs in hand— sweeping aimlessly at forever-falling leaves, some clearly a little weary, nodding off on the roadside… in all manner of positions.

I see people waiting for the bus, squatting in what looks to be the most uncomfortable of positions, but for this nation, I now know it's anything but.

Speaking of squatting… the nation's toilets no longer have me in a state of horror at the mere thought of having to use them. The frantic rummaging through my bag for tissues and hand sanitiser and deep breathing before entering the 'squatting vortex' has been replaced by a more low-key approach.

I hear the now-familiar tune of "It's a Small World" whistling from the back of a big truck squirting plumes of water across the road in an effort to spray away the settled dust that's blown in from the desert. I know it's definitely not the ice cream truck coming.

Firecrackers erupt into the morning air. There's nothing to see, but the sharp, crackling sounds that had me jumping out of my skin the first few times, now fade into the background like a distant rumbling in the sky.

I arrive at my destination, our daughter's international school. A kaleidoscope of coloured flags depicting at least a dozen different nationalities hang across the big iron gate. A security guard greets me with a big smiley "*Zao Shang Hao!*" (Good Morning) as we step into the schoolyard.

My driver waits while I settle my small person into class. Back in the car, the radio is alive with Chinese talkback—in between that and country and western songs from the seventies, we've settled into a comfortable ride. I can finally accept that 'small talk' is not the Chinese way. A simple '*Nihao*' and '*Xiawujian*' (Hello and See you this afternoon) will suffice. Even if I still have a desperate yearning to say, 'Have a good day' or 'How was your weekend (mate)?' I refrain.

Later in the day I'm walking in my 'hood... I see a woman holding her little girl over the gutter to relieve herself. I hear older men clearing their throats loudly, some spitting on the footpath. Whilst I still grimace inside, I no longer feel the need to screw my face up in a futile attempt to convey my absolute disgust and irritation at the situation. I understand it's a cultural thing. And that's just the way it is.

The fear of being run over, that saw me unable to cross the road in front of my house (to reach Starbucks), has subsided... I can weave in and out of the cars with more confidence and while crossing on a red light is still hairy I can safely do so with the rest of the meandering population.

A trip to my local hairdresser doesn't make me want to curl up in the corner when they all stare at me as if I've just landed from outer space. Most of them cannot speak English but when I hear Madonna playing over the sound system I can't help but smile. I am probably the only one who knows all the words to "Like a Virgin" and I make sure I sing it loudly, knowing it's the one time I have the upper hand in the language stakes!

In fact, the blatant staring at the white woman in the street no longer makes the hairs on my skin stand up... truth be known, these days I am giving as good as I get!

Any prior shyness and/or intimidation have evaporated as my curiosity piques and I'm constantly straining for a deeper insight into this fascinating nation of people.

Suddenly, one year in, there's an unexpected feeling of confidence, that you realise, until now... you've been sorely missing. Perhaps it's not a case of familiarity breeds contempt but rather familiarity breeds contentment.

While, there's no denying, living in China will probably never 'feel like home' to me... for now, it's my new 'normal'!

Somebody pass me the Tim Tams.

Australia

Here's a Tip on the Tip
Kristine Laco

My husband and I grew up in Northern Ontario, Canada. The furthest we had travelled was Mexico, and we stayed at resorts. It was a shocker to our families when we packed up our lives on the Wednesday following our September wedding and boarded a plane from Thunder Bay holding one-way tickets to Melbourne, Australia.

Exhilarating, nerve-wracking and terrifying were all words I would have chosen to use if I wasn't busy writing thank-you notes for our wedding gifts.

We arrived and jumped into everyday life. It was spring in Melbourne, and we had to learn to drive on the other side of the road, understand how to order a coffee and figure out where the best pizza was. It was an adventure every day. I needed to find a job while we also searched for a flat, a car and some friends.

When December arrived, I was working on a contract, and my husband was in the trenches too. We planned to spend one weekend doing what all good Canadians do in December, decorate a tree. We didn't see any traditional tree-yards as we would find back home and the Internet

197

wasn't yet in homes. We had to read—gasp—a local newspaper to find out there was a 'cut your own tree' lot only forty-five minutes from the city. We had our Saturday plan.

We headed out in our Ford Laser hatchback while wearing our shorts. We chose the perfect tree, felled it and strapped it to the top of our vehicle. On the way home, we collected as many stunned stares as one could gather and then lugged our holiday spirit into our flat. We had brought Christmas decorations with us from Canada, and the apartment was ready for the holidays.

The thing you may not think about when you cut down a tree in summer versus pick up a cold, bound tree in winter is that it is summer. It seems obvious, but when we brought that tree in the house, added the lights and then approached it to decorate, the bugs that inhabited our tree decided to come out for a peek. I'm a Northern Ontario girl, and the bugs are slightly, or maybe even dangerously, different in Australia than at home. I had never seen a bug in a Christmas tree, but I was about to get a treat. The charming fellow that crawled up my arm was as bright green as the Grinch, long and had huge bug eyes. That may seem obvious, but these eyes were huge and they bore into my soul.

Luckily he didn't bore into my arm, but I jumped and screamed. My husband, having not seen the menace, was perplexed, and we never saw that bug again. Three years we lived in that flat knowing that my Christmas critter inhabited the walls.

We never thought much about not seeing Christmas trees around. We were in wedded bliss and making the most of our new lives together.

We hosted a dinner party that December and were

proud to show our new friends our decorated flat. They had never seen a real Christmas tree. They had seen indoor potted plants used as decorations but never a tree. Our friends spent a lot of time admiring our decorations and, as we found out later, unwrapping our gifts because they kept asking for sticky tape.

January came and went, and we had no idea what we were going to do to dispose of our bug home. Our friends were of no help. Each day we would survey the rubbish room, the sidewalk and the storage area in the garage. Nothing. Everyone appeared to be keeping their trees alive in their flat for eternity.

One sunny summer morning in mid-February, we were heading back from the gym when we saw it. A Ute (half-car, half-pickup-truck called a utility vehicle or Ute, for short) carrying what appeared to be a load of rubbish. Included in his haul were some twigs, sticks and greenery that could have been a tree if super-glued back together. As a private detective on a mission, we followed the fellow and discovered the secret. Australia doesn't have garbage dumps or even rubbish dumps. They have tips. 'Tip' is the word for the garbage dump. That is why the *Yellow Pages* were of no use. This does not, however, excuse our friends.

My husband and I high-fived each other and knew the rest of our day was going to be stripping the decorations, secretly lugging the ridiculous lifeless tree out of the house and shoving it in the car.

When you have a tree up in an apartment for two months in the middle of summer with no air-conditioning, two things will be clear. You will not be able to get that tree out of the house without creating a large amount of mess, Hansel-and-Gretel style. Second, you will meet every neighbour you have never seen before in the process and have to tell the story about why you are stealing a dead tree from a flat. In truth, we didn't get past "G'Day" when our neighbours realized we were foreigners, so it worked out.

We made our way to the tip feeling very festive with our needle-less tree inhabiting our hatchback. We waited for our turn behind every Ute in town. We arrived at the front of the line to dispose of our Christmas remnants. The man working the yard gave one look, a snicker and said, "You sure you don't want to keep it 'til next year, mate?" Welcome to our new home.

North America

Are You an Expat If You Don't Know You Are?

Robin Renée Blanc

I was born, and lived the first seven years of my life, in St. Ann, Missouri—a middle-class suburb of St. Louis. We had a three-bedroom, two-and-a-half-bath brick house with a two-car garage on a quarter acre of land. The house was located on the corner of two cul-de-sacs so it was very quiet and safe. I had my own room, but my two older brothers had to share a room. Mom worked at Sears as a bookkeeper and Dad worked at Wagner Electric as a machinist. She worked days and he worked nights, so I mostly only saw him on the weekends. It all seemed normal.

I rode a bus to the nearest public school, Briar Crest, and usually bought lunch in the cafeteria. My favorite was the pizza burger! Also, when we had chili, it was always served with a peanut butter sandwich, so to this day, I have peanut butter bread with my chili or it doesn't taste right! Our lunchroom was the gymnasium the rest of the day, and we had mats for tumbling and basketball and things. Outside, we had a playground for recess, with monkey bars, tetherball, and other installed equipment as well as an athletic field for playing baseball and other field sports. We had music and art classes and a library. It never happened to me, but we all knew that the principal had a paddle to spank you with if you misbehaved. There was a bathroom on each of the two floors, with several private stalls and a row of sinks. All the students and teachers were white.

Mom always put me in dresses—those short little-girl ones that barely covered your panties. Since she worked at Sears, she got a discount, and anyway it was what little girls wore in the sixties. But it was SO cold wearing a dress in the winter! I asked her why I couldn't wear pants to school, since I wore them at home. She told me that girls wear dresses. I thought that was a stupid rule when it was cold and snowy, so I asked my teacher if I could wear pants. She seemed a bit surprised, and told me, "Of course you can." I told Mom what the teacher had said and wore pants from then on. The other girls started wearing pants too. I still rarely wear dresses or skirts. And I'm still a rebel.

When I was in the second grade, my mom left us to live in the Bahamas. I was alone with two high-school aged brothers, and a father who worked nights. I missed my mom, but my life seemed to be the same in many ways because I still slept in the same bed as always, and went to the same school with the same kids. Everything was familiar.

I went to visit my mom in Nassau during the Christmas holiday and at the end of my trip she asked me if I'd like to stay there. I was having fun, so I said sure! She lived in a one-bedroom apartment and we shared a big bed. She had a job working at one of the big hotels on Cable Beach. She enrolled me at St. Matthew's school and I started classes. I was put into the third grade, which was my age group.

Even though English is spoken in the Bahamas, it wasn't the same language that I knew back in Missouri. The first week at school, a girl in my class came over to me and asked to borrow my rubber. I had no idea what she was talking about. I remember throwing up my hands and looking down at my desk, asking, "What is it?" thinking that I didn't know what it was, but I apparently had one. She gently touched my eraser, and I said yes. She was a white English girl, but the majority of the students were black Bahamians.

Another difference in language was in the way words were pronounced. I couldn't really tell the difference at first, but the other kids laughed when I said 'cat.' They would laugh and tell me, 'Say cat.' I'd say cat, and they would laugh. Then I finally realized I was saying Kat, but they were saying kYat. So I learned to say it their way so I wouldn't be laughed at.

We went across the street to (Anglican) church every Wednesday morning. The girls had to wear scarves. Most of us had a scarf that matched our uniform, which was a gray canvas jumper or skirt, and a red-and-white gingham blouse. Only the big girls wore skirts, and I had a jumper since I was only seven, and I felt too warm. I saw a girl with a gingham dress, which seemed a lot cooler to wear in the heat, so I asked my mom if I could get one. We had to get a seamstress to make it (the regular uniforms were ready-made), but I was a lot happier. I noticed other girls got lightweight dresses after that too. Rebel again.

I had just begun learning multiplication when I left the US, but my new class had already learned their times tables. I was on the sixes in Missouri before the Christmas break, and with no more formal instruction, I never memorized the rest. If I ever have to multiply, I count and add to get the answer.

Other differences were the daily visits by food trucks at lunchtime, and ladies with tables of snacks in the dusty schoolyard, where we ate our lunch. I mostly took my lunch, and sometimes got candy from the vendors, usually a Blow Pop. I didn't like the chocolate much—Cadbury's tastes a lot different than the Hershey's I had grown up with! I learned to play marbles in the sandy dirt of the schoolyard, and I learned how to sing and play 'Brown Girl in the Ring', and handclap games. I only remember having organized physical education one time, and we went down the street to a kind of park/open area and played games. We had art class, but no music, no library. Girls had to do stitchery, which I thought was silly. I wasn't going to do the handkerchief assignment, but one of the boys brought in a piece of cloth for me to sew. He wanted to give it to his mother. We got teased a few weeks about it, but after that nobody seemed to remember. There was only one small bathroom without doors on the two stalls, and a sink. It was icky and I learned to hold my bladder all day so I wouldn't have to go inside.

The biggest difference from the US was that the teachers caned students regularly for misbehaving, which shocked me. But the other kids didn't seem to be bothered (of course, nobody wanted to get caned, but they found it 'normal'). The first time I was caned, I wasn't even guilty— a girl at my table talked, but the teacher thought I had. I was so mad! But after that it became routine. The boys usually got more 'licks' because they would act out more. I seem to remember that in third grade, they hit the backs of our legs, and then the next year, they would hit the palms of our hands. Either way, it stung!

Mom drove me to and from school at first, but then we

moved to a two-bedroom apartment closer to school and I walked both ways down Shirley Street. I went back a few years ago and that apartment was about a mile from the school. At the end of third grade, Mom asked me if I wanted to change schools. I had been on the waiting list for another school. It had only been five months, and I really didn't feel like having to start over again, so I decided to stay put. But after fourth grade, I knew the landscape better and I had met girls from other schools at church and that the other school was better, so I asked to switch.

In the Fall I started at Xavier's College. Xavier's was a much bigger and nicer school. There was a large field for sports separate from the playground, as well as a pool for gym class. I was put into Scholastica team or house—which was like a British prep school. There were only two houses—the other was Seton—but it made things easier when teachers had to split us into groups. I think we were blue and they were red. My new uniform was a white blouse with a pixie collar, a green criss-cross tie, and a heavy dark plaid jumper. When it got really hot, the boys got to loosen or even take off their neckties, but the girls still had to wear our ties, which really made me mad. Several of us tried to get to take off our ties in the heat, but we were told that it wasn't ladylike.

My grade was in their second year of French, so I had to catch up quickly, and with no help from the teachers. I asked if there was material from the first year that I could study but was told there wasn't any extra. It made me a little annoyed that I hadn't switched schools the year before when I had the chance. We had music and art classes, and I remember being part of a student show on the real stage in the school auditorium. Everyone brought their lunch and we ate outside on the same concrete area where we assembled each morning. There was a 'normal' bathroom on each floor like in Missouri.

Mom drove me to and from school because it was too far to walk, even though we had moved to a cute little villa behind the King & Knights Club that was closer to the new school. There was no caning at Xavier's and I didn't miss it. Also, there was more diversity in the student body. The student body was a mixture of Bahamians and what I now know are expats. Still, at that time I did not know what an expat was, let alone that I was one.

At the end of the school year, my mom decided to leave the Bahamas because of the possibility of unrest due to the new Bahamian independence in July, and to attempt reconciliation with my dad. My mom had had boyfriends while we were in Nassau, but I was so young I didn't think it was strange—it was just one more new thing to adapt to. My parents ended up divorced and Mom married a Bahamian, so I am now forever entwined with those 700 islands in the sun.

Wasting Away in Paradise
Stephanie De La Garza

After knowing I wanted to live in Central America for the past fifteen years, I decided to take the leap. I quit my twenty-three-year career, sold my house, cars, and almost all of my possessions to live in Costa Rica at the age of forty-three. I found a wild animal rescue center to volunteer for on the southern Caribbean side in the town of Cocles, near Puerto Viejo where I would be living for three months.

I had the ocean as my front yard, the rainforest as my backyard, and it was literally paradise. The sound of howler monkeys woke me each morning at 4:45 and my beautiful yard buzzed with hummingbirds all day long. The calm waves lapped upon the beach, which was my favorite way to walk to work.

When I used to work in an office, I'd say, "I wish I could work outside all day." Well not only would I be working outside all day, I basically lived outside. I sat outside, I ate outside, I read outside, I worked on my computer outside. I could hear the waves crashing on the beach while I was... outside. I could smell food cooking, people smoking and I heard them laughing, singing, and talking. I had no climate control. When it rained, everything got moist including my sheets, clothes, and books. The picture I had hanging in my room folded over at the edges and if I didn't dry my laundry in the sun, my clothes started to grow mold.

My kitchen was open to the elements and I had to secure my food in a large bin or in the refrigerator so ants and other critters couldn't get to it. I had to eat fast or the ants thought it belonged to them. I got used to having them in my drinks and eventually, I just saw them as protein. Large spiders were common, even finding one inside my blender one night. Geckoes were welcomed guests, often cowering from some of the larger insects.

Having sat behind a computer for over twenty years in the IT field, the physical exertion started taking its toll soon after I arrived. No longer did I have a car to drive, but a bike as well as my own two feet. The exercise was good for me, as was eating fresh fruits and vegetables and learning how to cook on a two-burner electric tabletop stove. No longer did I have the comfort of air-conditioning or a good bed to sleep in. The heat and humidity was stifling and the amount and size of the insects were enough to drive any sane person mad.

Each day at the rescue center was a mix of gardening, cleaning enclosures, preparing food, washing hundreds of dishes, and doing laundry by hand, along with monkey- and sloth-sitting. Constantly moving and being on my feet for six to eight hours a day found me hiking up my pants and looking for a makeshift belt. Stomach issues started to plague me and I became severely dehydrated with no desire to eat. I had brought my water filter with me and used it constantly, but wondered if the restaurants I would sometimes visit had made me sick. Being around animal feces all day crossed my mind as well, but I never went to the doctor.

As the pounds started coming off of me, I became lethargic and had to reduce the hours I was volunteering at the center by half. I looked and felt sick and I was losing weight quickly. In all of the years of traveling to Central America, I had never gotten sick before. I figured it must be temporary and would pass, but it didn't.

You could always tell who the expats were there. Very thin, gaunt, and although tan, they looked a bit sickly. I said to myself one day, "I wonder if that's what I'll end up like after a few months?" Sure enough, I was starting to fit in. You could tell who the tourists were by their healthy plump figures and happy faces. There was something going on here that I hadn't been let in on. When I talked to a neighbor about my illness, she said that everyone gets stomach problems on and off. She had lived there quite a while and said she still had bouts of diarrhea. It had to be the water or the lack of hygiene when preparing food, as I don't believe they have inspectors for restaurants. When you live in the tropics, all sorts of things thrive in the moist hot climate, so it was no wonder that things went bad quickly and you didn't know until it was too late.

My visa was coming due after being there for ninety days. When I arrived in Costa Rica, I was 120 pounds. About two-and-a-half months later I was ninety-nine. I went into the rescue center to work, eyes sunken and dark, clothes falling off and when the owner saw me, she said, "Do you want me to call a doctor?" She did and I left in tears, going to find the doctor's house. Unfortunately, he wasn't home. I went back to my *casita* and lay in the hammock sweating, hot and uncomfortable. I tried to eat something and drink some juice. I felt like dying and didn't even care at that point if I did. By the next day, I actually started to feel better and didn't go to the doctor. I only had a few more days left until I was going back to the US to visit before returning again to Costa Rica, albeit a different part of the country.

I made it to Virginia and met my mother at the airport who claimed I looked like a refugee from Darfur. However, I slowly started putting on weight again. I had sold my water filter to a friend back in Costa Rica and a couple of weeks later she informed me that it was leaking. The base of the filter had become separated from the part that held it together. This had been a known issue by the maker but it didn't occur to me to check it. So the whole time, I was probably drinking unfiltered water and that's what had made me so ill. With American food back on my plate and mom plumping me up, I bounced back with no residual effects. Would I do it all over again? Absolutely, but this time with a functional water filter!

Confessions of an Expat
Tina Celentano

It was 1978 and I was an aspiring young actress pounding the pavement of Toronto. I had just left an intensive acting school and my hopes and dreams were large. The siren call of Hollywood and the film industry was beckoning me westward. I couldn't help myself. I had to go. It was the opportunity to become someone different, lead a new life and yes possibly become famous. Who could resist that? And so I broke the news to my family, packed my belongings and headed west.

It sounds so romantic from this far in the future and I confess that it was. As Sinatra's iconic song of LA's sister city, New York, claimed, it was the place to make it if anywhere was and I truly believed this of LA. If I wanted to be a part of the film industry, this was the place. The motherlode. The golden ticket.

It's a blessing of youth to have so much optimism and faith in oneself. I just knew that was where I was supposed to be and in fact when I did arrive and settle in, I felt like I had come home. It was odd to feel so in tune with such a vast, strange place, but in LA I wasn't strange or out of place. LA embraced uniqueness, strangeness, oddities. It was all part of the theatre. Shakespeare had once written that all the world was a stage and that could describe LA completely. Phone calls and letters from home tried to lure me away but I couldn't leave. So much physical beauty in that city: the natural beauty, human beauty, art and architecture, music, and film, film, film. Sunset Blvd and the huge billboards, Malibu Beach, Santa Monica Pier, Burbank. I was hooked.

And yet as soon as I saw someone from home or at least anyone who said they were Canadian there was an immediate camaraderie. We were Canadian, we belonged to a special group, we were exclusive, we were cool. People chuckled at our quaint expressions and our accents. "We killed ourselves laughing"; "I'll have a coffee"; "Beautiful weather, eh?" It felt like I was straddling two worlds. I was at home in both and in neither. I was different but in LA everyone is different. It is why there is such a glorious melting pot of creative, quirky people pushing the artistic envelope in so many ways. Art. A life of art. An art-filled life. It was my magical kingdom floating in the mist. Yet there were so many times I was fully aware that the magical mist was really smog.

There was one event that bridged the expat gap. My good friend, a screenwriter, was hired with his writing partner to write for a Canadian TV series. They wrote several episodes and were invited to Toronto for a taping. That year my friend came home to Canada for Christmas and we spent a couple of days in the TV studio. It was marvelous. I was an actress, part of the industry. I had studied with acting coaches, read a myriad of books from both old and new acting teachers, sat in on professional rehearsals and was taught to dig deep into myself to find that creative spark inside. Yet I confess I also loved the trappings of that exclusive environment. I loved to be on a movie set or a stage. Lights, camera, action. Replay that scene again. I loved the sets, the makeup and the costumes. It was heady stuff. I worked on film, TV sets, in the theatre. I was a part of that creative, wild tribe.

It was so much fun but also so much heartache. Every role I played was named Maria. I was told that although my face was pretty I was too fat for television. Lose twenty pounds. Learn Spanish. Practice dancing or horseback riding or other accents. Get new headshots. Audition, audition, audition. One more callback but they went with the other actress. They liked the TV pilot but it won't get picked up by a network this time. My one big film scene left on the cutting room floor. Such a naive little girl from north Ontario. So much of her was still there.

And then I got tired. And then I got cynical. And I wanted something more. A husband, a family. An education. A career. But that was not back in Canada. It was right where I was already. So much of my heart was in Toronto. But I was a California girl now. I belonged with my feet in the Pacific Ocean. My soul would always long for the other place, wherever I was. And I was okay with that. A child of a larger world. Two countries, two minds. One heart. I have heard the philosophy that one cannot be loyal to more than one country but I have to ask why not? We are a global community with many different perspectives. How can I not want to be a part of it all? And so it comes to what I feel is at the heart of the expat. Idealism. The belief that home can be found in many places or maybe just one: within. I would not trade my travels, my adventures, those old dreams for anything. I did not become that famous actress or even a working actress but I found myself in so many ways. And I am so proud to be an expat living in the global community.

South America

The Making of a Brazilian Body

Brynn Barineau

"Just tuck the heart rate monitor under your sports bra. Just like that... good. Now I'm going to put the mask on. You let me know if it's too tight."

I nodded hoping I'd understood the Portuguese correctly as the trainer slipped a rubber mask over my nose and mouth and adjusted the straps behind my head.

"Okay, I'll keep increasing the speed every minute. You let me know when it gets uncomfortable."

When you're running on a treadmill, with a rubber mask and hose on your face, things don't become uncomfortable. They start out that way and proceed to get worse. Within five minutes I was running flat out, sweating underneath my rubber muzzle, and listening to the friendly blonde chat with my husband in Portuguese.

I voluntarily submitted myself to all of it. Although I hadn't known exactly what was in store when my husband and I were told we needed a physical evaluation before starting our new gym.

It was my first gym membership in Brazil. I'd been living in Brazil for four years but had always had access to fitness rooms through clubs. Now that we lived in Vitória, Espírito Santo, we needed a gym.

My gym-going in the United States in no way prepared me for the intensity with which Brazilians in Vitória approach fitness.

But let's dispel a big stereotype about Brazil right up front. Not all Brazilians look like supermodels. There are 280 million of them and they're not all between the ages of eighteen and twenty-five. People get old in Brazil. People get overweight in Brazil. People get too busy to go to the gym in Brazil and the effects show up pretty quickly in a culture that considers french fries an acceptable side to white rice.

The people who do go to the gym, however, are going to be people concerned about their health and want to look and feel good. I think that's true of any country's gym goers. It was very clear after our tour of the gym though that the Brazilians sweating and grunting through their workouts weren't interested in looking good. They were going for perfect.

The human body gets the worship it deserves in Brazil. With a tropical climate and 4,655 miles (7,491 kilometers) of coast, it's on display in many cities 365 days a year. The body is turned into art in both feminine and masculine forms during Carnaval. Tiny bikinis and speedos are appropriate for all ages and sizes. People have bodies. What's the big deal? My own ass is as white as the day I arrived in Brazil, but I appreciate the body acceptance on display.

Of course when bodies are on display all the time, the perfect ones do receive a lot of attention, and the competition for that attention is intense. Way more so than I was ready for. I didn't show up at the gym wanting to craft the perfectly shaped, bikini-ready bottom. I just wanted to maintain a decent blood pressure and mitigate the consequences of my sweet tooth.

Maybe I should have made that clear at the beginning because every new member at my gym goes through a complete physical evaluation. It details every problem area and is used by the trainers to develop your personal fitness routine.

My evaluation started with a series of questions. "Do you drink two liters of water a day?" (Does anybody?) "Do you smoke?" "What medical problems run in your family?" Then I took off my shoes and shirt to be weighed and measured. Marisa, our evaluator, didn't just take my height. She measured around my arms, legs, calves, waist, hips, ribs, around major muscles flexed and un-flexed.

I knew this was serious data collection when the calipers came out. Nothing brings you down like watching all of your body fat get pinched and recorded. I had thought I was in pretty good shape, but I began to doubt it with every notation Marisa made.

When Marisa finished cataloguing my fat, she asked me to stand against the wall, centered in front of a grid similar to that used for mug shots. Like a criminal, I got my picture taken: front, left side, right side, and back, but unlike traditional mug shots my pictures cut my head completely out of the shot. It was a mug shot of my butt. Wanted: my ass for being disproportionately large.

Despite feeling foolish while doing the tests, I left the gym glad to have done the evaluation. Isn't knowing your body's tendencies the first step in maintaining it? The trainer knows exactly what areas you can just maintain and if there are any you need to improve. The evaluation was a good idea.

Then I saw my mug shots.

My husband and I met with a trainer the next morning to have our results explained. I was all set to hear him explain my good results and tell me I'd passed my evaluation with flying colors. I'm certainly no Olympian, but I'd been going to the gym pretty regularly for years. I anticipated good results.

A trainer pulled up my results on a computer in the weight room. He took a second to skim the brightly colored charts. My Portuguese wasn't great at the time, but this is what I heard.

"Okay, your goal is to drop your body fat by 4 percent. You also need to increase your percentage of lean body mass. Your right shoulder hangs slightly lower than your left, which makes your pelvis tilt up on your left side. We're going to have to work on that. You really need to improve your cardio. The evaluator recommends at least thirty minutes on the treadmill a few times a week. We'll give you some ab exercises to reduce your waist circumference and of course we'll concentrate heavily on your glutes and thighs."

I was waiting for him to tell me I had a brain tumor to go along with my fat, scoliosis, and weak heart. Then he scrolled farther down into the report, and my butt mug shots came into view.

These were the most unflattering, complex-inducing, fat-roll highlighting pictures any human being has ever had taken. With the helpful grid on the wall behind me, I could measure just how far out my butt protruded from my body. My profile shot provided a wonderful comparison between the horizontal extension of my butt and boobs, which, being under a sports bra, were non-existent according to the grid.

Never once did the trainer say to me, "You're doing great in this area." I heard nothing except my current measurements and goals to work toward. By the end of the review, I believed I was guilty of assault every time I put on a bikini.

What exactly were my results? I've since had a child but at the time, I weighed 62.8kg (138.45lbs) and my body fat percentage was 18.35. The evaluation recommended reducing my body fat percentage to fourteen and losing 2kg (4.4lbs). To do this I needed to increase my lean body mass (muscle) by 1kg.

When the trainer gave me those numbers, I had no idea how they compared to other people. I'm not a nutritionist or a doctor. The trainer just told me how much fat I should work on losing. I was genuinely dismayed and believed I was, in fact, slightly overweight. Two hours of Internet research later, I learned that 14 percent body fat is the lowest amount of fat an athletic woman my age should have. A woman needs 12 percent just for her organs to function well.

The trainer really made me believe I NEEDED to lose the fat. I couldn't understand why he had said, "Your *goal* is to lose 4 percent body fat," as opposed to, "4 percent body fat is all you can lose and still be healthy." It's not a hard sell to convince women they need to lose weight. In my experience it's more difficult to convince us that we're perfectly healthy and can afford to enjoy a side a french fries. I was baffled and a little pissed.

My first day working out, I noticed the abundance of six-packs and unitards, and I understood. The trainer had just assumed I would be like the vast majority of the women at my gym: in pursuit of physical perfection.

The Brazilian women at my gym are the sexiest collection of gym goers I've ever seen. Their hair is long and flowing. Many use eyeliner for the occasion. It's like working out in a Flo Rida music video. There's more leopard print here than on a jungle safari. You can also see lots of paisley in all the colors of the rainbow. Every outfit is perfectly matched and accessorized with dangling earrings.

Many women avoid the risks of mismatching by going with the unitard. Before I started going to my current gym, the unitard was, for me, merely a myth. An extinct manner of dress that could be seen in historic records and frequently used in comedy sketches, like the toga.

I'm pleased to report the unitard is alive and popular here in Brazil. Surprisingly, there are quite a variety of cuts. You have very low cut backs that dip so far down it's possible to count every vertebra. Some have cutouts on the sides and others have lace-up backs. They also have fronts cut so low there's no way the woman can lift her arms over her head without everything popping out.

But lifting one's arms is something most of the women at my gym never need to do since 95 percent of their workout focuses on legs. Probably to pull off their unitards. And boy, do they pull them off. In addition to being sex bombs, I'm pretty sure every woman there is also a triathlete. These women sport six-packs and perky, round butts without any jiggle.

I'm not exaggerating when I say every woman at my gym is hardcore. From time to time, I scan the gym specifically looking for anyone who could stand to lose a pound or two. I'll see maybe four or five. Everyone else looks like an athlete and this includes the grandmothers in the room. My first week at the gym, a woman who couldn't have been younger than sixty followed me on the squat press and upped my weight by 40kg. It was a very humbling moment.

I was more than a little intimidated by the overt sexiness of the women during my first months at the gym. The women are sleek, styled, and fit. I'm usually in baggy shorts with my ponytail askew. In the end though, I decided a ponytail is better than sweaty hair clinging to my back. For me, comfort trumps fashion, but I will take a cue from my Brazilian sisters' commitment. These women, of all ages, have made exercise an integral part of their lifestyle. They run. They lift. And they're not afraid to be strong. That, unlike unitards, is something worth imitating.

What Mattered Most
Sally Rose

Unless there is a protest or a football match, Chileans tend to be solemn people. They don't show much emotion in public.

Among close friends and family, they can be as loud, silly, and as spirited as anyone else, but that usually stops when they leave the safety of home.

A student in one of my first English classes adopted me as her "American Mom" early on, and I was often invited to her home for birthdays and special events.

On a sweltering December day in Chile, I had been invited to her high school graduation. It was to take place at the school in the evening.

That day, I had another commitment. I was baking all day in a hot room with no air-conditioning, common in Chile. As the project dragged on later than expected, I watched the clock tick.

Nothing was going to prevent me from making it to Francisca's graduation on time, but before the graduation, I still needed to go home, shower and change, and then buy a bouquet of flowers for her.

I was finally dismissed at 3:30. It was late, and I was too tired and frazzled to walk back to my apartment, so I jumped in a cab.

At home, I cleaned myself up and changed, before rushing back out to the Flower Market across the Mapocho River.

It was late in the day and many of the flowers looked wilted from the heat. Pickings were slim, but I chose the best of the worst.

I must have overdone it because the bouquet turned out to be an enormous armful of flowers.

Rather than take the metro, I once again got into a taxi, which sped away from *el centro*, south to Barrio Franklin.

When I climbed out of the cab in front of the school, only a few people were milling around, most of them vendors selling flower bouquets, toys, and other graduation trinkets.

As people began to arrive, they bought bouquets as they went in. Their bouquets paled in comparison to mine, and I didn't know whether to be pleased or embarrassed at my ostentatious offering.

Francisca and her family had not yet arrived, but rather than wait around outside, I got into the line of parents and started moving forward, toward the entrance.

I got as far as the reception table, which was set up inside the gate. There, they asked for my invitation. I hadn't received a written invitation, but I explained which student I was there to see graduate.

"You must have an invitation to enter." They sent me back outside the gate.

I couldn't believe that they wouldn't allow me in. After all, why would a random *gringa*, carrying a garden of flowers, try to attend a graduation if she weren't connected to one of the students?

Chileans were sticklers for rules, so it was no use arguing. Without that piece of paper, I wasn't getting in.

Francisca and her family showed up soon after. I entered with them, and she convinced the gatekeeper to allow me in as part of her family, before going off to find her classmates.

We took seats in the first row behind the graduates. Mom, Dad, Grandma, best friend Jeni, and I sat as close to the stage as we could get.

There were hundreds of girls graduating, divided into three groups. For each group, there were separate speeches, awards, and diplomas. The Chileans applauded politely after each turn.

Finally, it was time for the general awards ceremonies, where they awarded prizes for "bests."

As they were about to announce the Best Score in English, Jeni leaned over to me and whispered, "Francisca's going to win this."

"Do you think so?" I asked.

"Absolutely. She has seven points."

I suddenly had an idea. "If she wins, we're going to stand up and cheer." I told Jeni. "Tell her parents and Grandma."

Jeni stared at me as if I'd lost my mind.

"We can't do that."

"Why not?" I took in the quiet, seemly applause, and I knew why. Chileans didn't behave that way. It just wasn't done.

"She will never win this prize again. It's a time for real celebration. If she wins, we're standing up! Tell her parents."

Jeni turned to her other side and relayed my message.

Francisca's family all leaned forward to look at me as if I'd grown a second head. I nodded at them and lifted my hands in a "Well? Are you with me?" gesture.

Reluctantly, they nodded back and gave me a thumbs-up sign.

Seconds later, when the school director did indeed call out Francisca's name, we stood as one and applauded wildly, cheering and whistling.

The Chilean families around us had looks of shock on their faces as they stared at the crazy family who had dared to show that much emotion in public.

But the only face I cared about was Francisca's as she stood on that stage and watched us, grinning from ear to ear.

No Fixed
Address

How Not to Say Goodbye
Catriona Turner

It was around midnight, but still warm enough to sit outside the Irish pub in the French town on this early summer evening. My leaving night had taken us from the hip café-restaurant in the old town, via a relaxed wine bar, to here, where we chose a table beside the boulevard, looking out towards the mountains, for 'just a couple more'. There were seven of us: the stayers and stalwarts. I took in my friends' happy faces as they chatted, feeling very at home, shiny with wine and company, half-raised my glass, and announced, "There's something I want to tell you..."

It had been only about three years since a house party with friends had marked the end of our first posting in the same French town. In fact, that first posting, at a full three years, remains our longest to date. So some of the friends we were celebrating with had become our family, those friends we're still regularly in touch with, who we still make plans to meet up with from different corners of the world, whose new babies we will soon be holding. Although we were saying goodbye to them, it was really only 'until we're on the same continent again...' But with others, I was at the bottom of a learning curve about how not to say goodbye. I was hearing myself, at that party and at other final coffees, playgroups, dinners, saying something all too often: "I wish we could have hung out more."

(Wait... I said that out loud to people? How very un-British of me! Clearly I was already on this learning curve. How else could I have so earnestly expressed a desire for time in another person's company?)

Well, I really was saying it, sometimes to people who'd only recently arrived in town, but more often to really cool people I had known for a while, but with whom the opportunity for closer or deeper friendship had somehow passed me by. In those moments, I was inwardly making a resolution to notice the opportunities next time around, to not be saying goodbye that way again.

I reflected on how this had come about. I thought back to first meetings with friends and acquaintances. There were moments where it was quickly clear that friendship was blooming. Is it weird to remember what a girlfriend was wearing the day you met her? At our company's first social event couples were split up into different teams, to maximise mingling. The girl standing beside me was wearing a tartan skirt and black heels. We nervously commented to each other about the activity we were about to take part in, laughed together, and the conversation was relaxed from there on in. Later, as we drifted towards our respective fiancés, we discovered they'd already homed in on each other as compatriots, and were chatting easily about 'the old country'. Couple friendship sealed. Two years later I made a 15,000km-round-trip in a weekend— five months pregnant—to be at their wedding. Another time we went bowling with a friend who was introducing us to the girl he hoped to persuade to join him in his expat life. She wore a sexy green wrap dress, accessorised with such fun and confidence that I immediately developed a huge friend crush. Last year our children played together in Paris. These are the friends, among many others, who we now count as family.

But what about those really cool people I hadn't hung out with enough? What had happened? In the early days I still had a more 'permanent' social mindset. Friends-of-friends were just that, part of someone else's circle, why would that change? Making small talk with a fellow partygoer was just something you did at parties, and it would be rude to start interrogating them with 'big' talk. Not to mention presumptuous to imagine they'd want to tell you, or feel the need to get to know you better. Such was my pre-expat (and probably very British) mode of socialising. Little did I know that the thoughtful, beautiful girl whose name was an ocean and was way out of my friendship league, was the one who would make me cry at our leaving party. I didn't realise that the ladies' man in the centre of a group of blokey blokes on the other side of the room would become a colleague with whom I would closely collaborate, and on whose behalf I would be bursting with excitement when he finally met The One. What is somewhat true in 'real' life is intensely true in expat life: every seeming passing acquaintance is a potential friend for life.

So that was my first lesson in how not to say goodbye: drop the casual prejudices, and be open to every new friendship from the start.

Before I joined my husband on our second posting, I had to go home for a little while (pregnancy... Africa... vaccines... blah blah blah). But even this detour from the expat journey helped me understand how my perspective had already changed. I spent most of those months staying with my in-laws, the main benefit being that my toddler could play with his cousin in the same village, while via my sister-in-law I'd have instant access to the local mummy network. But my access wasn't to be as instant as I thought. I was a newcomer—just a visitor, really—in a village where many of the other playgroup mums had already spent their entire lives, and although others were new to the expanding community, they were settling into 'forever homes'. They'd all be hanging out together fifteen years hence. No urgent need to rush into friendship here. In my first few weeks everyone was polite, helpful and friendly, but while I expected my second playgroup arrival to be met with an encouraging *Cheers*-style chorus of "Hi!" the minute I walked in the door, they were, very normally, taking their time to get to know me. And probably feeling pretty uncomfortable with my expat-style "where-are-you-from-why-are-you-here-how-long-have-you-been-here" questions. Several months later I definitely had a new group of friends—we'd been out for dinner together, I was even given a thoughtful leaving present. But I'd had to work at it... and be patient!

So lesson two was: remember to appreciate the depth and intensity of expat friendship.

Finally arriving to join my husband on our first African posting, I was ready to be open-minded. (With the huge advantage that Sexy-green-wrap-dress and her now-husband had been sent to the same place and were living two floors up!) Before arriving I'd joined a local expat network on social media, so within a couple of days I posted my plea: "New arrival seeks mummy network for regular morale boosting." I quickly had an invitation to join a playgroup with a group of international friends.

Those weekly gatherings soon became my touchstone, crucial to survive and negotiate the bewilderment of African life as a parent. But at that time I was also starting to crave the kind of friendship I'd been missing for years: the BFF, the girl who just gets you, who always wants to do the same stuff as you, with whom you'll have at least one guaranteed laughing fit whenever you meet. Even though I've concluded that such friendships are rare gems, and even though my true BFF these days is the one I married, it's still always worth seeking out. I'd quickly identified that the laid-back, slightly-punk Dane who'd originally invited me to join their group was a really cool person. I was right—on our occasional group dinners she and I were the ones who were last home, putting the world to rights over one last drink at the bar. At one point she revealed that she didn't often invite new people along, but she'd had a hunch about me... I definitely wanted to hang out with her more.

Here was where I started to realise that 'hanging out' is not as simple as it was when I was a student twenty years ago. Time with friends these days is structured around playgroups and play dates, which are endlessly interrupted by little voices, or else tends to be a lunch or dinner in a large group, with new arrivals, of course, welcome and included. Daytime get-togethers are always constrained by clock-watching for pickup time, and weekends are focused on the family. Spontaneous 'hanging out' has to be worked into the schedule.

With just a year left of that posting, this truth took a while to dawn on me. I was joining in as much as possible, taking every opportunity to meet new people, be open to the possibilities, but was limited by my own lack of effort to schedule things the way I wanted them to be. Our stay there ended even sooner than originally planned, and I found myself saying once again to my laid-back, slightly-punk Dane, among others, "I wish we could have hung out more."

Thus, lesson three: join in, but make your own magic happen too.

Once I knew we were heading back to the same French town we'd left two years previously, I was at an advantage—several of my friends and contacts were still there, so I could hit the ground running in my quest for hanging out time. And I really had to, as this time we were only expecting to be there for a few months!

Another interesting factor gave me a head start: the People I May Know. Yes, thanks to a certain social media site's determination to be at the centre of our lives, I could get a sneak preview of potential acquaintances. Creepy confession time: I couldn't resist clicking through where mutual friends were in the same town, to go full judgey judgerson on the profile photos of strangers/future friends. Needless to say, more casual prejudices abounded. (Although I did get one or two things right...)

One particular 'People I May Know' was involved in the playgroup I would be rejoining. The first time I saw her from a distance, arriving at a family event, I recognised her as one of my sneak previews, the one who was probably X and Y, who I probably wouldn't have much in common with, wouldn't be hanging out with much... Lesson one fail. Luckily, it only took a couple of playgroups to discover that she wasn't just really cool, she was awesome. She had the quality of utter honesty and directness that I've always found irresistible, I had at least one guaranteed laughing fit whenever I was with her, we always wanted to do the same stuff... it felt giddy, like being a teenager again. Even better, the feeling was mutual.

But I'd arrived in May, was still settling in June, then, this being France, there were two full months of long summer holidays with travelling, visitors, lots of visitors (because, south of France...) and no routine whatsoever. My time was running away, and this time I was agonisingly aware of it. In September, *la rentrée*, life was getting into full swing again... but I was due to leave in January!

Out one evening, over a bottle of wine or three, a group of us, awesome new friend included, realised that we were all interested in sewing. The Brits among us eagerly tried to explain the concept of *The Great British Sewing Bee*, and why it had become download-by-any-means essential viewing, to our German friend (there's a challenge). Then the idea formed. Why not have our own sewing bee? Once I'd insisted we call it anything other than 'sewing bee', we made a plan. Happily, we picked the day when my older son had an after-school club, so no clock-watching. The three of us who had little ones in tow reckoned that they would, at least some of the time, entertain each other. We got together at around 10 a.m. at one of our homes, figured out how to plug in five sewing machines from different countries with minimal electrocution risk, and gathered enough nibbles to see us through until mid-afternoon. Then, we just... hung out. For most of the day. Bliss.

We aimed to do it fortnightly—which was over-ambitious—but managed at least a monthly get together. I can't say I did much creative or productive sewing; I was mostly getting through my to-be-taken-up pile. But we shared our hacks and resources, while conversations meandered into areas there wasn't usually time for. We shared expectations and frustrations, stories about our families and extended families, and revealed the people we were before we took on the mantles of expat, spouse, parent. We'd created for ourselves a sanctuary.

And I'd learned lesson four: claim the people, claim the time.

Spring came, and our stay was extended until the summer. The expat gods (the HR department) had granted me bonus hanging-out time. Until six months ago, outside the Irish pub in the French town, glass half-raised, when I told my friends a story. I told them about how I hadn't wanted to say goodbye with the phrase, "I wish we could have hung out more." I told them that there were people I'd met who I'd quickly decided I didn't want to say it to. And I told them that those very people were all sitting around that table. I told them I was grateful, but also proud, that this time I'd made it happen. We all raised our glasses. This was a good goodbye.

Yes, Me Too!

Rosemary Gillan

I have been contemplating the picture on my computer's desktop all morning. It's a plump garlic bulb with a clove of garlic missing and a segment of orange sitting in the space where the clove should be. Yes the orange pod fits perfectly into that space, but something is not right, for it does not belong there.

I know what that orange segment feels like. As an expat who has moved on average every eighteen months and lived in eighteen cities in fourteen different countries, I learned how to fast track an outward appearance of assimilation but I never quite captured the intricate feelings of belonging.

Now that I am repatriated back into my home country, I find that I am still every bit the outsider, a person wanting desperately to belong.

This feeling of not belonging goes back to my birth in India. If the United Nations were a nationality, I could claim to be a citizen, though parts of me are perhaps not so cohesively united. I was the child of mixed race parents— Scottish, Portuguese and Indian on my father's side and

German, Irish and Indian on my mother's. As an 'Anglo-Indian', I never felt like I belonged to my birth country, being caught in a limbo of neither being recognised as Indian, nor wanted by the British who sired our sorry race in the first place. My father aided and abetted this non-compliance of belonging by constantly berating the land in which we lived and promising to move us away, anywhere from this 'bally' country—to England, Canada, the States… and eventually he did, to Australia.

So we moved to the red-necked Brisbane of the seventies where our brown skin put us at odds with our ever-so-English behavior, and again we were the Misplaced Race, forever needing to explain how we could speak English and yet come from such a 'backward' country as India. We breathed a huge collective sigh of relief when dad found a job and moved us to Sydney. Finally, civilisation and no questions asked to our accents or skin colour. Maybe, just maybe I could belong here.

But Sydney turned out to be the launchpad for my expat life. It was here I met and married at the tender age of twenty, a hotel man whose career admirably suited my belonging-challenged identity. For the hotel business is accommodation on the run, a career choice perfectly suited for the restlessness within which my soul comfortably resided. Within the next few decades, we had two children on the move between hemispheres, leaving one challenging zone for another, either unpacking or packing, getting to quickly know, embrace and love our host country, and then just as quickly decoupling (quite like the 'conscious uncoupling' of Martin-Paltrow celebrity) and moving on to repeat the same exhaustingly emotional cycle in the next host country.

Along the way the marriage faltered, shaken severely in

parts, stirred gently in others. What kept us together was the constant moving, a gravitational pull that hugged us to the sides of the whirling expat world we inhabited. This constant repositioning kept us together, distracted us from the personal, threw us into the communal. We grieved each country we left, while secretly hoping for a new start—in both a marital and cultural sense—in the new country.

The loss/hope feeling is the same in each new host country with each stay bookended with the same two emotions: grief and excitement.

Let me explain the grief. Expatriate friendships are quite unlike the ones back home. As an expatriate, we don't have the luxury of time to get to know someone, so the moment we arrive, the clock starts ticking. Our average stay was less than eighteen months so in that short time I learned to embrace life in the new country by joining every club, church, and cultural group, taking up membership in anything and everything, and latching onto and starting close relation-ships with any person with whom I have the remotest amount of commonality—i.e. I'm living in their country or we're both expats.

This is now my new family. With locals, I try to become a local myself by finding out more about their country, particularly where they eat, shop, visit. Being very interested in their cultures, their festivals and their history, I ask a million questions but go a bit easy here as culturally I have to tread lightly until I understand what the 'no go' areas are and where I can freely speak my mind. With expats it's different. Within hours of meeting someone, I'm sharing intimate details of my failing marriage, missed pregnancy and feelings about eternity. I get down and dirty, it's the only way to survive. Over share. Spread the grief. We expats help each other by saying, "Yes, me too!"

So by the time I leave, expats I've met during the last eighteen months know more about me than my decades-old friends (and very often my own family) back home in Australia.

Those personal attachments are not the only ones I grieve. As I tend to embrace life wholeheartedly in each country in which I reside, I develop a strong affinity with my host country, forming a strong bond with its arts and culture, its food, the idiosyncrasies of the nationals, its enclaves, its towns, its coasts, its plains. From an expatriate's point of view, I gather plenty of information on the best schools, local restaurants, hospitals, medical clinics, hairdressers, foreign supermarkets, dentists, grocers, spas, stores and tailors, not to mention the main tourist attractions in that city—country, if it's small enough—so that I can be a very willing provider of free accommodation and tours for the many family and friends who are bound to soon arrive on my doorstep.

I very quickly get familiar with the culture, the language, the people. My heart gets tightly wrapped in my host country; it feels like being in a cocoon, covered in a colourful web of attachments both personal and cultural. I am now a 'local'. I learn the slang, walk through local areas, sample street food, hang out with local friends and go on hair-raising rides on the back of scooter-taxis, eyes wide shut, fearing the terrain but loving the adrenalin. I feel wildly alive. How could I ever live a 'normal' life back home again? I secretly ask myself.

But now it's time to leave for the next host country. I weep as I say farewells to my expatriate and local friends alike. The tears carry me on the plane, drip down the sides of my face, pool in the hollow of my neck. I have belonged for a while, but it was just that. A temporary belonging.

Across hemispheres and sideways, from south to north, east to west, we move. Australia to England, back south to Argentina, across to Chile, north to Turkey, down to the US, further south to Mexico, across to Singapore. Pause for a family break-up in Sydney. Deep breath, grab that glimmer of hope and work hard at the resultant reunification in Nepal. Then across to the United Arab Emirates, south east to Vietnam, and finally north to China, where the whole sorry marriage finally falls apart and this mum and her two little kiddies cry wee, wee, wee all the way back 'home' to Australia.

But home to what? Repatriation is so much harder than expatriation. As an expat you're given grace to be a foreigner and total strangers move mountains to help you acclimatize to your new location. An instant support network is born of non-judgmental people whose only commonality is that they've been there, they know what it's like. "Yes, me too!" they sympathize. We're all in this together, as the song goes.

But repatriation? I come home to my old hangouts where nothing has changed. Problem is, I have. I now look at life through wide-lensed eyes and a softer, kinder heart. I'm more tolerant, small things no longer irritate me; I have seen a bigger picture and cannot unsee the things I've seen. I've visited villages where poverty and happiness sit together just as comfortably as wealth and misery do in my first-world home city. I'm no longer an insider back home, I'm an outsider looking in.

I join expatriate networks, people like me, 'misfits' all, except they are the 'real' expats, foreigners in my home country. I'm the 'local' now, and the day it dawns that I no longer fit in there has me in open-mouthed shock. I turn to Facebook where my 'other' community awaits. There I can talk to my hearts content with expatriate friends who are in the same boat, repatriated home and feeling lost. We all understand, and like we did back in our host countries, we say again to each other, "Yes, me too!"

But this online community is one-dimensional. It's a flat screen 21" TV after an I-MAX experience. How can it ever compensate?

So I look for the novelty where I live. I become a tourist in Melbourne, take an online course, sign up for Internet dating (and sign out very hurriedly soon afterwards), join a gym, start Ceroc dance classes, paint and drink wine, together, with not-too-disastrous results.

As a Christian, I search and find a multicultural church. Ah. Thank goodness for that source of guaranteed community, the balm that helps soothe the tattered edges of my identity. I look around and feel at home among the Asian, European and South American faces. And I wonder why I always gravitate towards foreign faces, languages, foods. That sense of being with kindred-foreign-spirits touches my heart.

I start to think about my fear, my unease of being 'home' in Melbourne. I think about the countries where I felt a sense of belonging and see that where it lay was the expat scenario of the unfamiliar. The strangeness of things calms me and makes me feel at home, makes me belong.

I sit up with a start. That's it! I feel comfortable when I am in the unfamiliar. Now that I have returned to the familiar I feel uncomfortable. I feel totally displaced being here in Melbourne. And it occurs to me that this is the first time ever that I have returned to the same place, the same house even. I am so out of my comfort zone.

My daughter's Art Project from her final school year comes to mind and makes me smile. She painted a map of the world on a large canvas, flicking specks of paint on all the countries in which she grew up. The city of Melbourne, Australia in the far south-east corner of the map was marked more prominently than others. Here it was that she was born, and here she had excitedly returned when her expatriate school days were over, eager to get to know it as 'home' for the first time.

It worked for her. As for me, I wish I could be sure that Melbourne is truly my home. Will I file away my past so that I can fit into my present? After all, that is what I have done all my life, fitting into the present world I was in. Now my present world is my home city, a setting not strange, nor different. Dare I get used to being comfortable in the familiar?

But something is missing here. My children have grown up and left home and no longer need me like they once did. My husband has since remarried. Heck, even the family dog has gone, a victim of a weak heart at a grand old age.

And so I am alone at the crossroads of my future, longing, like ET, for home. I so very much want to be wanted, to belong, to say, "Yes, me too!" to all the lucky ones who can identify their forever home. So I will park my expatriate history in a suitcase and store it on the far corner of the topmost shelf of my heart, take a deep breath, and dive into my present.

The Evolving Vocabulary of the Expatriate Life
Akajiulonna Patricia Ndefo

The contrast between my growing up days and those of my kids is very distinct. In my case, I grew up in my home country of Nigeria. I went through one school for primary education, another for high school and another for university. I had mostly the same friends all through each of these phases and, aside from our local language, we all spoke English, as taught by our parents and teachers. Yes, there were the occasional holiday trips for summer vacations, but home was the base we always returned to. So there were no real challenges to adjust to, or changes in vocabulary.

Fast-forward several years, when I decided to pitch my tent with my hubby and very quickly I realized that ours would be a family on the go; one in constant motion.

We moved within the first year to another state within our home country, and moved house twice while in that location. It was then our turn on the conveyor belt of expat service. Those moves all happened within four years and two pregnancies! No easy feat!

Truth be told though, I had been looking forward to this expatriate life. I love the thrill of adventure. Getting to see new lands, exploring different cuisine, appreciating new cultures, making new friends and perhaps learning a new language. I always saw it as a wonderful opportunity.

I am now a mom of three adorable kids and unlike myself, my kids are slightly confused as to where home is exactly. If you asked them this question you would get varied answers. My first two kids would say Netherlands, but my third, although Dutch-born, would say France. The confusion is understandable considering that in the space of five years 'home' has been in three countries.

In all of our moving around so far I realized that I have had to learn (or re-learn) from my kids, new versions of words I had already known my whole life.

For example, in our new 'home' in Canada, no more are they toilets, or restrooms, we now say washrooms. I still need to get used to that because I find myself telling my son to take clothes to the laundry room, which I sometimes called the 'washroom' because, for me, that is the room where our clothes are washed. When I say this he asks repeatedly in confusion, "Mummy, the washroom?" until the light bulb goes off in my head and I realize my mistake and correct myself.

We are experiencing our first winter here in our new Canadian home and this has brought new names of cold weather items for me. Gloves are now mittens, and hats are now toques. One of my Calgarian friends still chuckles when she hears me say cardigan. It's a lot to remember but I'm determined to get a hang of it.

As a football-loving family, there are Saturday mornings when my son is up at 5:00 a.m. to watch the English

Premier League matches live. Thankfully for PVR, I am gradually convincing him that we can record the match, sleep in and watch it later. What is interesting though is how quickly it has gone from 'football' to 'soccer'.

As we move along with our ever-changing vocabulary, I now know it's not always so much a case of learning new or different names of items, but the influence of the culture and the spoken language in the country we were living in over the years. For example, while in France my daughter who attended a French daycare knew taking a nap as *'fais dodo'* usually with a *'doudou'*, which is what French kids call the stuffie they sleep with at bedtime. Potty training for her had some French influence as well because for her to go I had to ask her if she wanted to *'caca'* which was short for *'faire caca?'*—an informal way of asking if she wanted to do a poo. She wouldn't go if I said it in English.

Learning they say never ends, and so far I can attest to this being true. I am continually learning through the evolving vocabulary of my globetrotting trio. So far it has been an enriching experience and I'm curious to see where my vocabulary heads next.

The Ripple Effect
Angie Benoit

St. John's, Canada – June 26, 2006

When choosing our new fur baby, Ripple, we looked at our decision-making from all angles but missed one major factor—life would happen! And a short six months into life with our stubborn, black, cute-as-a-button Shar Pei, we were offered and accepted the opportunity to become expats. We positively embraced the thought of living in a new country and knew that Ripple would be by our side for every step.

At first we got a lot of chatter from family, friends and acquaintances: "What will you do with the dog?!" "You can't take Ripple!?" "How can he go?!" Then the never-ending list: microchip, vaccines, shots, blood work, titration test, air transportation that all seemed a bit overwhelming at first glance. But day by day and little by little we checked off one task at a time and before we knew it we were on our way. Ripple as excess baggage!

Stavanger, Norway – May 2007 to Sept 2008

The flight from Canada to Norway was a long, eighteen-plus hours. Perhaps too long without a potty break. So, arriving in Stavanger in the early morning hours set the perfect backdrop for an escape attempt. Not quite. He just needed to find his way outside the airport terminal to do his business. To this day my husband still talks, with amazement, about how a little puppy could hold so much fluid.

Ripple's escape attempt didn't stop there and despite his prior obedience training he was still stubborn. One evening my grand efforts of persuasion to get him to come back inside after sneaking through an open door completely failed. I ran up and over a mountain and through the forest to catch the free spirit. I came to an end at a farm. Cows grazed in the field but no Ripple. A farmer appeared and signed with his hands "five" by holding up five fingers, next he put his pointer finger to his temple and said, "Boom"… my heart skipped a beat. Then in his broken English said, "Marry." Luckily, my husband was in the house at the time of the escape and watched me disappear over the mountain. He was quick to the thought and drove around the mountain to arrive just in time to catch our crazy dog chasing cows. My 'marry' was a hero and saved Ripple twice that day. Once from getting trampled by a cow and second from being shot by an angry farmer.

Our time spent in Norway was short and sweet, wild and free even. We did a lot of firsts and new-to's. New expats, first-time pet owners and doing our best as expats with our fur baby.

Pet travel within the EU is friendly. You are just required to carry an updated pet passport. Off to the vet I went to get a puppy passport. It was supposed to be that easy. In fact it was easy until the movers came and I told them to pack everything in the room (puppy passport included). I screamed when I realized what I had done, but it was too late to find it. I found myself paying an emergency fee to get a duplicate passport of the one that had just been completed days earlier.

Esbjerg, Denmark – Sept 2008 to Jan 2013

The transport to Denmark was quick. Just an hour's flight. Made easier if you push your luggage trolley carrying a large kennel, with dog, through the 'Nothing to Declare' line. No one stopped us and maybe it was a sign for the time to come.

Life in Denmark, with a pet, was easy. Beach walks, forest treks and city strolls were the daily highlights. Then one cold afternoon in December 2009, we added a little boy, Magnus, to our family. Ripple accepted Magnus into our home without losing a moment's sleep. He continued to snuggle down into his bed, on the floor, at the foot of our bed night after night.

The longer you stay in a country the harder it is to leave. The moment you relax, let your guard down and make lifelong friends, is the day your husband arrives with that dreaded question… "Would you like to move? What about Africa?"

"I will never live in Africa." "Ripple will die in Africa!" In disbelief, for two months, I repeated these statements daily. Meanwhile, Ripple could care less where in the world we lived as long as we were all together. Smart Dog!

Pointe Noire, Congo – Jan 2013 to…

It was a long two days of travel. Late afternoon departure from Denmark, connection via France, to fly through the night for an early morning arrival in Congo. Of course there was drama at Paris' CDG… isn't that normal!!??

Ripple never made many major adjustments, until now, to enjoy his expat life. He was born and lived within the always-changing four seasons, was a regular at the '*Hund Pension*' (Dog Kennel) and culturally welcomed.

All that changed when we landed on African soil.

Being an expat for six years by now, it somehow felt new again. Adjusting to the never-ending heat, Ripple became happy to stay inside with the air-conditioning. Not being an outdoor dog... his outside explorations were limited to the four walls of our fenced villa in five-minute intervals. There was no longer the easy access to a kennel. Instead, Ripple made friends with our house '*menagere*', Reine. Reine cared for Ripple during family vacations. Ripple and Reine quickly became the best of friends. Culturally... not only was having a dog as a pet foreign to the Congolese it was also foreign to many of the other nationalities present in this large expat community. Many friends refused to visit our home as they were either scared of dogs or too uncomfortable to have a dog touch them. The Congolese were scared... doubly scared of a 'black' dog. Ripple quickly accepted his new role as watchdog and used his 35kg weight to his advantage. Because of him, our perfect little family felt safe, settled and at home in 'unsafe' Africa.

Two-and-a-half years passed quickly. The struggles life threw our way in the early days was now, somehow, 'normal'. Ripple aged. His history of skin issues, along with internal and topical tumours—cancerous—became more than his lungs could handle.

Sadly, Ripple said goodbye to us at the age of nine, on July 17, 2015.

This dog was my constant. Countries changed, languages changed, cultures changed, but Ripple never did. He was always there; a steady companion in the times where I'd left my old friends and had yet to make new ones. Our addresses have changed, and the walls of our homes have followed suit, but Ripple never did. He was the only life I knew, no matter where in the world we lived. Transitions were made easier because of him, and now, six months later, I still struggle to find my way in our expat life without him.

When Going 'Home' Isn't a Clear Choice

Jennifer Hart

There it is. The moment has arrived and you are a bundle of excited, nervous, giddy and overwhelmed energy. Either you, or your significant other has been offered an opportunity that will take your life as you know it and transplant it into a foreign language, culture and environment. You can't help but let your mind wander. Depending on where you're moving, you might be imagining yourself sipping coffee on the Champs-Élysées, or if your destination is tropical, you picture yourself spending every afternoon on the beach. You become slightly intoxicated by the exotic promise of the adventure in front of you. Yet, the reality isn't escaping you and panic starts to set in. There will be challenges. You may have to learn a new language and learn to re-communicate again as an adult, even if it is an English-to-English location assignment.

Making the choice to break from the life you had in full-motion is not an easy one and comes with significant ramifications. The unofficial rule of thumb is that the positive or negative ramifications depend on a few things: your approach, how quickly you make other expat friends and how adaptable you are. I know because I have been there several times over.

In 2005 I made the decision to follow the love of my life (now husband) to Paris, France. From the outside it seemed like a no-brainer. Move to Paris and sip coffee and champagne at Café de Flore every day? Yes please!! Yet, it was so much more complicated than that. Parisian life was amazing in so many ways but it was tough. Meeting people and creating a social life was extremely hard but it did eventually work out through my love of sports and the eventual arrival of my two Paris-born children. The language, while not a problem for me in general, became a noticeable barrier between the local French-speakers and non-French speakers, such as myself. I had an accent, which meant every day for ten years I was asked where I was from and how long I would be visiting and what the duration of my stay in Paris would be. I was polite in the early years but eventually learned to reply, "It's been X years and I think I have forgotten to leave!"

During the Paris years, there were discussions of possible relocations to China, Dubai and even the beginning stages of relocating back to my husband's old job in the UK. None of these panned out for various reasons, but living with the constant threat of a new country, new life, new friends, new language, new everything began to wear us down, especially as we didn't feel settled where we were.

Once you move overseas, you slowly, without noticing at first, start to develop a new struggle around your identity that you didn't know existed before. Before your move, you had simple answers to questions such as "Where are you from?" and "Where's home for you?"

Changing your life, your language and your culture puts a chink in that chain of answers and living in Paris epitomized that for me. Paris wasn't my first international relocation but it was the one that changed me the most. Being treated like a tourist daily weighed heavily on me. After being gone as long as I had been, I somehow reached a point where I no longer felt like I belonged back in Canada, yet clearly didn't belong in my new home. I had a British passport thanks to my mother, a Canadian upbringing thanks to my birthplace, an English husband, two French-speaking children and not one clue of where I considered my 'home' to be! I longed for that to change. My heart began to search for something more permanent that fit the cultural and linguistic mash-up my family had become. All of these reasons resulted in our move to Switzerland.

Yes, it is true that my husband received an amazing job offer, precipitating our move here, but there was more. For at least three years prior, we had been having what I call the 'expat talk.' Similar in discomfort to any deep 'where are we going in our relationship' talk yet unique to multilingual, multicultural and multi-confused families. We decided the time had come to start looking for a more permanent home for our little family. Since my husband and I are not from the same country, we have struggled with this conversation. We do not have a common 'home' or culture that we both yearn to go back to. We have met many same-nationality couples and are always astounded by the inherent and collective knowledge that one day they will go 'back home.' We don't have that. You would think that would exempt us from the familiar pressure questions such as, "When are you moving back home?" but it doesn't. Whose home do we choose? Whose family should we be closer to? What side of the Atlantic is better for us? Either choice still comes with the annual need to make an international trip just to see family. We saw many positives and negatives for both sides of the world, his home country and my home country, but there just never seemed to be a simple and clear choice between the two. There was, however, an external choice that increasingly pulled at our heartstrings.

The truth is, we chose Switzerland long before it chose us. We listed off the things that mattered to us personally and for our family. We wanted to blend the Canadian-Franco-Anglo life that defined us and start a new chapter. It was scary for us, being quasi-nomads, to start thinking of a more permanent living situation but we were ready. Switzerland, living up to its reputation as being notoriously difficult to get into, put us through the ringer. Three years we waited, stressed, cried, came 'THIS CLOSE' and finally, it happened. We moved here as locals: no more decisions being made for us by someone else, no more expat contracts, no more: "When your contract is up in eight months, where will we be living?" We moved 'home' in a sense that can only make sense to a family with no prior strong concept of home. We chose to settle down in a place we had never lived before. It sounds risky but it fit our version of normal and that is what matters the most.

So here we are. I am learning a third version of French, which I wasn't aware even existed. Canadian French was useful for me, if not patronized in France. France French is useful, if not laughed at a bit here in Switzerland. My brain struggles some days, but for the most part (and I do mean the most part) this is proving to be the right choice for us.

We all have something we want here and despite the incredible expense of Switzerland, the lifestyle has grabbed us and given us a big cuddle. We have settled here faster than any other place we have been before and that means something. We are locals and our benefits are NOT what they used to be but if you know Switzerland, you know we are doing just fine coming off the expat wheel. This is my fifth country and the one I choose daily to call home. That said, on game day, my heart will always be maple leaf-shaped.

Choices

Janneke Muyselaar-Jellema

May 1989. For most people it was a normal day in mundane life. This was not so for everyone. In the suburbs of Bulawayo, Zimbabwe there was a nineteen-year-old young girl frantically trying to fit the last things into her bags. Between the last-minute packing were the last-minute goodbyes. The car was leaving for the airport so there was little time to spare. Her viola would be part of her hand luggage; her tennis racket was strapped onto the viola so that it would accompany her too. Her parents, brothers and sister would all see her off at the airport. Of course there was a last family photo in front of the map of Zimbabwe. This was a historical moment.

The nineteen year old was leaving home. She was leaving 'the nest', spreading her wings and flying out into the unknown! She was the firstborn so she was the one to pave the way for her siblings. So with her head up, and gathering all her earthly belongings, she was going to board the aero plane. On the pavement heading to the plane the strap of her bag broke, obviously her bag was not designed for the amount she had piled into it. Was this how the rest of her journey would go? In front of all the people she was once again stuffing her belongings together to make it to the plane in time. One last quick wave and she was out of sight. The engines started; it was time for take-off. One last glimpse of the ones she loved, of the country she loved, of everything that was so well-known to her. Before she could stop it tears streamed down her face. Not just a few tears, it seemed like a dam wall had broken, causing a flood. Something like the Victoria waterfalls in rainy season. The tears were uncontrollable.

The past week had been busy and filled with goodbyes. There had even been a leaving party, with school friends and friends from the church youth group. They had had a lot of fun, there had been lots of laughter but there had also been the painful goodbyes.

This was the country where her family had lived the past six years. Here she had cycled to school daily, she passed her driving test, she had received her first kiss, her first dance, her first date, she had turned eighteen, been a school prefect and she had written her 'O' and 'A' level GCSE exams. This was the continent where she was born. Here she had learnt to walk, run, play, and laugh.

It all started long ago. Her father, the son of a farmer, came from the north of Holland. Her mother came from Delft. He went to study in Delft; they met, fell in love and got married. Her parents chose to live a life not for themselves, but for the benefit of others. They chose to live abroad. He had to do compulsory military service but instead he could go to a developing country and teach at a mission school. So the young couple left their homeland and settled in Zambia.

Then one day their eldest daughter was born. She was born in a mission hospital somewhere in the bush. The first white baby ever to be born there. When she was born there were no grandparents who came to see her when she was a few hours old. No aunts and uncles came bringing presents to her mum's bedside. It was warm. Her mum had problems understanding the Polish nuns and they had problems understanding her mum. The mother did receive a very special present: a live chicken! The little baby girl was baptised in the local church in the capital. Her grandparents saw her in real life for the first time when she was three years old. Of course they had seen photos and heard stories, read letters, but this was different.

The father, head of the family, always said we have to be able to listen to God's voice and follow his leading, so we must be ready to move to a new town or country if necessary. We must not stay too long otherwise we will grow roots somewhere. So the family moved from country to country, from town to town. All their children were born abroad. They grew up abroad. They grew up bilingual: school was in English and at home they spoke Dutch. In the holidays there were compulsory Dutch lessons not much enjoyed by the children at the time, but later much appreciated. Luckily the parents did not want the children to go to boarding school, so most of the time they were able to grow up close to their parents. Luckily the mother had a passion for family and could create a real home wherever they went.

There is a difference between a real home and a house. In a house all the furniture is in place, the boxes are unpacked and everything is neat but the family has not yet really moved in. They eat, sleep and move around in the house but it is not theirs yet. In their thoughts they are still in the previous country, the conversations are about old friends, old times and only the past. In a home even if the furniture is not in place yet there is peace and harmony. The family is together eating toast for breakfast as always, moving around the boxes, making jokes, laughing, and playing games. A home is where children flourish, wherever the home is.

Little did they know that this girl, their firstborn would travel back to her place of birth, back to her roots at the end of her teenage years, back to see where see was born and where the first three years of her life took place.

Little did they know that many people would wonder about her second initial 'Z'. They would try to guess her name, but nobody could guess it because it was a local name, a special name, one given by her parents and one especially from her country of birth. To this day on her passport under 'place of birth' only the mission's name is filled in, it does not say in which country it is.

Little did her parents know that years down the road when that little girl had grown up and wanted to get married that she had to contact the local authorities in her country of birth before she could get married because the birth certificate did not have a stamp on it. Months went by and money had to be paid before the official documents arrived and before the wedding ceremony could take place.

Little did they know that her childhood years would influence her career choice. She became a medical doctor so that years later, somewhere in the future perhaps, she will go globetrotting. It even influenced her partner choice. He was born in Holland but his mother came from Indonesia. He had travelled the globe: Thailand, Indonesia, Malaysia and Venezuela. That was one of the things she liked about him, that he had been abroad and that his life had not only taken place in Holland. His parents had even lived in Venezuela for a short time.

Little did they know then that during her university days and for seventeen years in a row she would choose to live in one house, one town, and one country and not move at all. She wanted to grow some roots somewhere. She did not know if she was able to do just that but she wanted to try.

As a medical doctor her childhood travelling influenced her place of work. She chose to work in an asylum seekers' centre. She really enjoyed being surrounded by people of many different cultures. Her primary school had been an international school, in her class there had usually been more than ten different nationalities at one time. Daily she worked with interpreters: Arabic, Chinese, Somali, Dari, or other languages. The asylum seekers came from many different countries such as: Afghanistan, Iran, Iraq, Somalia, Ethiopia, Sierra Leone, China, Albania, and Sudan. Now she did not have to travel but the 'world' passed by her desk. It was a challenge and a joy. Challenging were the terrible stories of what people had endured. It was a joy to look out of her window and see the children playing. Maybe these children had witnessed war, guns, the raping of their mother, hunger and thirst, but at least they could still play. There is a powerful force at work in children. They can adjust to a change of culture, country and language faster than adults can. Children have the power to play. Daily all the children went to school in the centre. The school was the centre of 'life'. There you heard the children laughing, singing, chatting and reciting Dutch words. Some children had never had the opportunity to go to school. The children were sad when it was Wednesday afternoon because then the school was closed. The atmosphere in the school echoed 'hope'. The children forgot their problems for a moment when at school. It was amazing what these teachers accomplished; they had a lot of patience and taught Dutch to these children, who all spoke different languages. The school was the favourite place for the doctor to go to too.

She knew a little what it was like to come from far away and try to adjust to a life in Holland. She had been nineteen years old when she left Africa, the continent where she was born and had grown up and went to study in the country where her parents were born. She looked very Dutch, blonde hair and blue eyes. She did not feel Dutch but nobody could see that. She spoke Dutch, but with an English accent. She pronounced the 't' too softly. She was meant to fit into university life just like everyone else. She was meant to do the things others did, say the things others said. Little did they know that her parents were thousands of kilometres away and that she could not visit them every weekend. That she only spoke to them once a week on a short telephone call. That she missed her family, her friends, her church, and her life.

Now the doctor, her husband and their children go to an international church. The preaching is always in English, which feels very familiar for her. She feels at home with people from many different nationalities. Church was always in English in Africa, so the English bible was much more familiar than the Dutch version. To this day there are moments that she speaks English with her siblings, her brothers and sister. Normally they speak Dutch to each other, it used to be compulsory at home when they were children. Now they occasionally speak English to each other just because it feels so familiar. It feels good!

In Africa she knew she wasn't African and she thought it was because she was Dutch. Now, in Holland she found out that she is not really like the Dutch people either. Where is home? She remembered that her younger sister had asked that questions years ago. Her sister decided that 'home' was where her bed was.

Of course, I am the girl who became a doctor in this story. I am the one who was born abroad. I am the one that looks very Dutch, with long blonde hair and blue eyes. I am the one who was called 'the foreigner' at secondary school. I am the one that did not quite fit in.

In the beginning it was difficult. Looking so Dutch but not knowing how to weigh the fruit and vegetables in the supermarket. I remember looking to see how others did it. How do you use the buses and the trains? Were the supermarkets open on public holidays or not? Sometimes I asked questions, but people would look at me and you could hear them thinking, "How can she be so ignorant?" Which brand margarine should I buy? Some days I chose not to buy chips because the choice was so overwhelming. I was used to one brand with a few different tastes. There was just too much choice. Even more difficult was: What clothes do you wear and what must you buy? Because I was used to school uniforms all my life. As a young child my mother always tailored the dresses, she even did the hairdressing. Fashion: What did I know about that? Once again the choice of clothes was overwhelming. Let's just skip that and keep wearing what I had. There were no holes in it yet...

Once I was invited to celebrate a fellow student's birthday on a Saturday evening. So I dressed up and put my best clothes on. For my grandparents' wedding anniversary I had gone on a shopping spree with my aunt. I had bought black trousers, a shiny blouse and two large necklaces. These were my best clothes. I added some make-up and I was all ready for the party. On arriving I discovered that I was a little overdressed. It was so awkward; I wanted to turn around and return straight home. No one else had dressed up. Everyone just wore their jeans. When someone celebrates their birthday here, it is with coffee or tea and cake, and everyone sits in a circle, talks to each other and then has another drink and leaves. It was a student party so we all sat on the floor. It was painful to discover that I did not know the cultural code. I had to start all over again. I had to discover what people meant when they said something and to discover how they celebrate happenings.

During my university days I helped start up a local international student organisation, to help foreign students feel more at home in their university town. For my medical studies I had to do a research project and again I chose to do it outside of the Dutch borders. The research was done in Edinburgh, Scotland. It was great to hear English and Scottish and to be surrounded with international students. It felt a little like 'home'.

There was something strange during my first year at university. It was as if I was older than my fellow students. I had seen more of the world. I felt that I had seen poverty and riches, health and sickness, life and death. Does that sound a little arrogant? Some of the students had moved for the first time in their lives when they went to university. It was hard to keep track of the number of times we had moved. In the book *Third Culture Kids* by David Pollock and Ruth van Reken, they describe it as early maturity. TCKs often feel more comfortable with older students and that was true for me too.

To me the students in Holland seemed so privileged. They received a student grant. They all seemed to have a CD-player; many had TVs and video recorders. Some had new cutlery, new dishes, and even new furniture. Dutch students did not seem to appreciate or be grateful that they had the opportunity to go to university. This seemed to have become a 'right'.

There are some things that became special to me when I lived abroad. Toast with marmalade, lemon meringue pie, trifle, marmite and potluck meals all had special memories attached to them. Memories of good times far away. The above-mentioned foods are not at all typical Dutch foods.

We now have a daughter, the little baby girl who was born in Holland. As one of her parents was born outside of Western Europe our daughter is entitled to a special vaccination programme. It is different from what the 'normal' Dutch children receive. The choices her grandparents made years ago to live far away as missionaries affect her life too. It affects the next generation. This is a small example but there are many more ways that her life is affected. Choices we make do not only affect our lives, but the lives of our partners, our friends, our family, our children and even our grandchildren.

Recently I have started reading about Third Culture Kids and I am starting to think about the journey in life that I have made up to now. Reading has brought back memories and provided lots of food for thought.

I think that being a TCK—or actually now I have to say being an adult third culture kid (ATCK)—has definitely enriched my life. Looking back on my childhood there are many fond memories, lots of exciting experiences, many interesting people and moments of adventure. I actually would not have wanted to miss it all. It is sad that I will not meet many of these people again, though in the age we live in the Internet provides endless possibilities to stay in contact with old friends.

I have discovered that it is important to talk about these

experiences or to write about them. Reading on the subject, I now realise that there are many more young people all over the world with similar experiences. I am not the 'odd' one out. I am not the only one.

Lost and Found Between Homeless and Homeful

Amel Derragui

Throughout my nomadic life, there have been two questions people asked me in every country I moved to that made me feel quite uneasy: "What is your mother tongue?" and, "Where is home for you?"

I still don't know how to answer these questions honestly without going through a whole explanation of my life history and current situation. Even then, it is still confusing to really define where is home for me and what is the language I relate to most. Sometimes, when I don't have the time to explain, I just say my home is Algeria and my mother tongue is Arabic, although I have only lived four years as a child in my country of origin, my "passport-country", and I am not quite as fluent in Arabic as I am in English or in French.

Before going any further, I guess I should now tell you everything about my background... For once, let me try to truly answer these questions without going through every single chronological event of my life, and let's see where it takes us.

Hmm, tough exercise…

Here is the thing, I don't have a home. It is as simple as that: I am *homeless*. I am a *serial migrant*, a *global nomad*. I do not have *one place* that I fully relate to. For me, home is a moving concept, which is probably a contradiction in terms… I often say that *home* is where I am at present, but the truth is it is not. It really becomes *home* only once I've adjusted to the new country, city, environment, culture and its people. By then, I usually have to leave and restart all over again.

Although I have never experienced anything else than this nomadic lifestyle, I struggled for many years from a lack of stability in my life. As I associate *home* with the notion of *stability* and *familiarity*, I felt *homeless*.

Once I reached my mid-twenties, I needed to build this stability and familiarity. So I tried to settle down in one country where I had built strong ties and friendships, but also a career. One of the measures I took to do so was to search for an apartment to buy. As I never had a childhood room, I needed some walls to own, walls that would represent my own borders; borders that I could cross without the stamp of strangers deciding on my fate.

Visa and *residence permit*… the words that hunted me all my life… I sometimes feel very vulnerable that my presence in each country has to be thoroughly documented, has an expiration date and is conditioned to factors that are not solely in my own hands. I feel like my whole existence has to be constantly justified. In these circumstances it is difficult to feel totally secure in the countries that become so much part of my life.

So what happened with my decision to settle down in the country that I had chosen because of my friendships and career? Well, I met with Love, another nomad, the exact opposite of what I was looking for. Sometimes the universe seems to know what is good for us better than we do... I met the man of my life and in no time he became another 'home' to me. With him, I feel safe, stable and in a sort of familiar place as we now explore together each country we move to.

When people ask us how we met (you might now finally have a slightly better hint of my background) he says, "It is the story of an Algerian girl, born in India, raised in Serbia and Uganda, living in France who meets an Austrian guy in Iran at a Turkish party."

Having found this place in his heart and having made space for him to settle in mine, I can finally fully appreciate all the other homes I have, even if each one of them represents only one portion of my whole identity. Algeria is where my big and loving family lives. All over the world is where the other most important people of my life are—my parents and brother—who keep traveling the world. The US (Utah, California and Arizona) is where I started my early adult life, developed my sense of entrepreneurship and made unforgettable human encounters. France is where most of my longtime dear friends come from, where I have built some of my beliefs and started a career. Austria is where my hubby and his parents come from and where we once fully furnished an apartment together. New York is where we currently live, making it our new home.

Today, I can define *home* as the place I identify with, and I identify with more than one. Each one of these homes completes my identity and makes it so rich. I am *homeful* and I feel so blessed.

Acknowledgements

First and foremost, to the wonderful women whose combined stories have made up the pages of this book—thank you for sharing your experiences.

Un grand merci to Lizzie Harwood of Editor Deluxe for being copy-editor extraordinaire! You've been my go-to girl throughout the project and you didn't miss a beat. You've made the distance between Paris and Borneo feel non-existent.

My expat friend, fellow teacher, and writer, Catriona Turner, your eagle-eye' skills in the early stages of me receiving stories was gratefully appreciated. Thank you for always knowing where the commas go! To the most avid reader I know, Lorraine Webb, who was always happy to peruse anything I sent her way.

To my Mom, Patsy Stadnyk for hand delivering the proof copies of this book to me in Indonesia and being its first reader. Also to my neighbour on the compound, and contributing author, Carole Clark, for being a wonderful 'proofer' and ever keen to remind me when it was time to stop for happy hour.

Finally, thank you to my family for their patience with me during the making of this book, as I passionately poured myself into my laptop for hours on end—ignoring the fact that we had a move to a new country on our horizon, again. You are my *why*. Girls, always be brave enough to try because that's when amazing things happen.

About the Contributors

Camille Armantrout, An Unbelievable Bus Ride

Camille Armantrout lives in rural North Carolina with Bob, her husband of twenty-odd years. They were lured there by a group of like-minded progressives, many of them farmers who value the simple pleasures of local food and community. Seasoned expats, Bob and Camille have lived and worked in Belize, China, Guam, Nicaragua, and Ghana.

Camille recently co-authored *Two Brauds Abroad: A Departure from Life as We Know It* with Stephanie De La Garza. A memoir with travel tips and advice, *Two Brauds Abroad* was crafted from a year and a half of correspondence between Camille in Africa and Stephanie in Costa Rica. For more information please visit: twobraudsabroad.com.

Brynn Barineau, The Making of a Brazilian Body

Originally from Atlanta, USA, Brynn Barineau has spent the last decade in Brazil navigating a multicultural marriage and raising a bilingual daughter. After years of teaching high school economics and explaining the US Federal Reserve to Brazilian teens, Brynn decided to pursue writing, an only slightly more daunting career. Her essays on expat life, parenting, and anything that warrants a facepalm can be found on BrynninBrazil.com. She's a passionate advocate for more diversity in children's literature and to that end, is currently querying agents for her first young adult novel, which deals with issues of multiculturalism. You can follow Brynn along the humbling road to publication with The Slush Pile, a humorous and brutally honest podcast detailing her attempt to publish a debut novel. The Slush Pile is available both on BrynninBrazil.com and through iTunes.

Angie Benoit, The Ripple Effect

Angie (Loder) Benoit had the great privilege to grow up in the small outport community of Cook's Harbour (then approx. pop. 250), Newfoundland Labrador, Canada. A world away from her trailing spouse lifestyle that she has embraced for the past nine years.

Angie knows that so many animals are left behind when their owners choose a travelling lifestyle. She smiles when she thinks of the wonderful life she was able to provide Ripple.

In this book, Angie's first publication, she proves that this exciting lifestyle is possible, doable, enjoyable and sometimes more beautiful when shared with our beloved pets.

Together, Angie, her Newfie husband and their six-year-old, Danish-born son are ready to take on their next country!

Robin Renée Blanc, Are You an Expat If You Don't Know You Are?

Robin was born in Missouri, USA and grew up bi-cultural, shuttling back and forth between her father's home in St. Louis and her mother's home in Nassau, flying on her own since the age of seven. This early exposure led to her love of travel and learning about new cultures: a French Club trip to Quebec in junior high; a high school exchange student in Brazil; a college junior term abroad in Vienna; and traveling to South Africa in grad school, the year after apartheid ended.

Robin earned a BA in International Studies and a master's degree in International Relations and has been an active volunteer with AFS Intercultural Programs since her return from Brazil. While teaching ESL in Japan, she experienced first-hand the transition from the Showa period to the new Heisei period. She is currently living back in Missouri with her two cats, Greta and Riley. Find her on Twitter at @RobinSTLMO and at robinstl.wordpress.com.

Margo Catts, The Land of No Logic

Margo Catts was born and grew up in Los Angeles, where one of her earliest memories was of hanging on the airport fence watching planes take off. International travel waited until children were raised, but after choosing travel over air conditioning one year after another, the dream of living overseas finally came true with a move to Saudi Arabia. She works as a freelance writer and editor, and her first novel, *Among the Lesser Gods*, will be published by Arcade Publishing in the spring of 2017. She now lives with her husband in Denver, Colorado, where she still looks overhead and wonders where the people in that plane are going. You can find her on Instagram and Twitter as @margocatts, and follow her blog at margocatts.com.

Tina Celentano, Confessions of an Expat

Tina Celentano is a Canadian expat from Toronto who currently lives in Washington State with her husband Rachid Tahiri, a Moroccan expat, and their cat, Archie. Their two adult children, Alexis and Bianca, live in a nearby city. Tina began life as an expatriate in 1978 when she followed her dreams to Los Angeles. A college academic advisor by day and a writer the rest of the time, Tina blogs about her perspectives and lessons learned in love, life and parenting from the empty nest. She loves travel, film, music and tea in the Sahara. You can read more of her writings at babyboomermomblog.com.

Carole Clark, Le Bonjour

Carole has been travelling around this planet since before she can remember. When she was just eighteen months old, her parents packed up their belongings with her in tow and moved from their home in Switzerland to the wild plains of Western Canada. Since then, she hasn't been able to quit and has made her home on three continents, first as a student and now as an expat. Needless to say, all this travelling has given her some experience to reflect upon, and plenty of material to write about.

Recently, she contributed an article to *Kula Magazine*, Bali, about travel and her other passion, Sophrology, which will be out in June 2016. You can read more at livewithpositivity.com.

Carissa Cosgrove, Coming of Age in the Middle Kingdom

With decades of writing gathering dust in beautiful wooden chests, "Coming of Age in the Middle Kingdom" is Carissa Cosgrove's first published piece of personal writing. An avid traveller, she has navigated 638,185 kilometres of the globe, according to her map on Trip Advisor. She does not have a blog, but regularly thinks about starting one—usually at three in the morning. Instead, Cosgrove is a lone parent to one lovely and creative little boy and the owner of FastWarren Communications; a business dedicated to providing high quality, efficient communications services to small businesses. A j-school graduate in a small town, she has most recently given herself to the dream of periodical publishing. Her newly divined publishing house Armagh Press will deliver the first edition of her magazine *#YGK Inc.* in the summer of 2016. You can find her at fastwarren.ca, by email carissa@ygkinc.ca or on Twitter @MsCGrove.

Cecile Dash, Diary of a Mom in Congo

Cecile Dash is a full-time career mom, who put aside her professional career three years ago when an opportunity presented itself for her family to move to the Republic of Congo. Living in Central Africa has been both challenging and fun, and Cecile quickly established a new life. She began keeping a journal from the first day and has now shared some of her writing in this book, where she makes her debut as an author. Cecile continues to share her writing and experiences with the world through her blog supermomabroad.com.

'

Shannon Day, A Man from Another Land

Shannon Day is a Canadian story-maker and cocktail-shaker. She and her family now live in the Toronto area, after spending a decade sipping tea and eating scones in her husband's "land." Shannon is a regular contributor for BLUNTmoms and has been published in various other online publications, as well as in print. Shannon is co-author and editor of popular book/martini guide, *Martinis & Motherhood: Tales of Wonder, Woe & WTF?!* Connect with Shannon over at martinisandmotherhood.com, or on Facebook and Twitter.

Stephanie De La Garza, Wasting Away in Paradise

Stephanie De La Garza from San Antonio, Texas was an IT professional for over twenty-two years when she decided to quit her job and sell just about everything she owned to live in Costa Rica. She worked with wild animals at a rescue center on the Caribbean then took on a house-sitting job near Turrialba. She then moved to El Valle, Panama where she helped a couple start a butterfly tourist attraction. Deciding to then go to New Zealand, she worked on a sheep farm followed by heading to Australia to check off items from her bucket list. Stephanie traveled back and forth for a year and a half between both countries and but is currently living in New Zealand after gaining a one-year extended visa.

Amel Derragui, Lost and Found Between Homeless and Homeful

Amel Derragui is a serial nomadpreneur and the founder of Tandem Nomads, a podcast show (online radio) dedicated to help expat partners take the leadership of their lives and build global portable careers. To listen to these inspiring podcast episodes and find great tips and insights go to: tandemnomads.com.

Michelle Estekantchi, Returning Home

Michelle Estekantchi worships her son and loves her husband. She is a stay-at-home mom who used to have a fabulous career that she sometimes misses. She also enjoys fashion, all things glossy, as well as a heart-to-heart, soul-searching conversation. She likes to live by the ocean and thrives in the sun. A citizen of the world? Maybe. She's definitely a local in many cities around the globe.

Parts of "Returning Home" have been previously published in *Knocked Up Abroad: Stories of pregnancy, birth, and raising a family in a foreign country* by Lisa Ferland and are reprinted with permission.

Leah Evans, Transition Woes in Ukraine

Leah Moorefield Evans moved abroad eleven years ago and has since lived in Georgia, Ecuador, Ukraine, and Paraguay. She is the proud mother of four fantastic expat children and runs the blog afterschoolplans.com, which provides resources and ideas for expat families regarding education and transitions. She has published *On the Move Kids, A Relocation Workbook*, a picture book called *Patches, the Moving Bear*, and was the editor for *Raising Kids in the Foreign Service*, a book of essays by a wide variety of authors. You can find these books and more at afterschoolplans.com.

Ersatz Expat, A Celebration of Problems and Resolutions – A Very Expat Christmas

Ersatz Expat is a thirty-something global soul, a perpetual expat. She has been a working expat, trailing spouse and expat child; born in the Netherlands to a Dutch/Irish family. Other destinations have included Norway, the UK, Nigeria, Turkey, Venezuela, Kazakhstan and various locations in Malaysia. In her early years, Ersatz Expat travelled with her parents and sister, these days she travels the world with her husband, three children and three pets. In 2016 the family moved to Saudi Arabia, her eleventh international posting.

Rosemary Gillan, Yes, Me Too

Rosemary Gillan is profoundly thankful to Dr Ruth Hill Useem whose coining of the term "Third Culture Kid" finally established her identity in the multi-cultural mix into which she was born and the life which was to follow.

Growing up in India as a child of Scottish/Indian/Portuguese/Irish/German bloodlines, she migrated to Australia with her family in the seventies. Within two decades, Rosemary met and married a hotel manager and thus began the Serial Expat lifestyle which took her to twelve countries over sixteen years, having two children along the way.

Writing tongue-in-cheek newsletters about her expat adventures to friends and family back home brought many requests for them to be turned into a book and after a slow start in 2013, Rosemary is now into the fourth chapter of "Tales of a Hotel Wife and Other Stories from Hell". "Yes, Me Too!" is her first published work. Find her on Facebook at Write.SaidRose and on Instagram at @rogjpix.

Jennifer Hart, When Going 'Home' Isn't a Clear Choice

Born and raised in Thunder Bay, ON, Canada, Jennifer has spent the last fifteen years searching for a place in the world to call 'home'. Having previously lived in the US and UK, Jennifer settled in Paris, France for ten years with her British husband, two Paris-born children and their Labrador retriever. When life threw a curveball in 2015, they found themselves packing up and heading off to Switzerland to start the expat experience again. Jennifer began blogging about their upcoming move and adventures at domesticblissabroad.com and has continued to write about life, family, travel and culture in Switzerland. Outside of writing, Jennifer is an avid runner, skier and professional packer.

Lizzie Harwood, A Paris Job Ain't All Macarons

Lizzie is the author of a travel memoir: *Xamnesia: Everything I Forgot in my Search for an Unreal Life* plus fiction: *Triumph: Collected Stories* and *Go See the Kids*. Growing up in New Zealand and PEI, Canada, she then lived in London, Rome, Sydney and 'Xamnesia' (haven't heard of it? read the memoir!), settled in Paris for 16 years, and is now in the land of ABBA—Sweden—with hubby, two girls and fluffy cats. She is an editor and writing coach to authors around the world. Find her at editordeluxe.com and lizzieharwoodbooks.com.

Marcey Heschel, Colours That Do Not Exist

Marcey Louise Heschel is a Canadian mother, wife and therapist living abroad in Kuala Lumpur, Malaysia. She and her growing family moved from Canada to Texas in 2012 due to her husband's career. In 2013 she gave birth to a little Texas Star named Sophia and in 2015 they relocated to Malaysia. Marcey spends her time as an expatriate raising Sophia as well as seeing clients at a marriage and family therapy practice. With an undergraduate degree in anthropology and a graduate degree in counseling, she has found a niche counselling people of varying ethnic backgrounds. She recently started an expat support group for struggling spouses dealing with relocation stress and anxiety. She is a loving mother and wife, passionate therapist, avid traveller, half-marathon runner and advanced scuba diver. She enjoys writing about her adventures, travels and cultural experiences on her blog marcey.me. Follow her on Instagram and Twitter @missmabes.

Kristine Laco, Here's a Tip on the Tip

Kristine Laco is a writer, storyteller and badass. She is the author at mumrevised.com and has been successfully keeping two children and a dog alive in Toronto for quite some time. Before children, Kristine and her husband lived for three years in

Melbourne, Australia where she never met Hugh Jackman. In her spare time, you can find Kristine binge watching TV, oversharing and embarrassing her teens by taking selfies at the gynaecologist's office and posting them online. Her middle finger is her favourite, and she lives by the motto that if you are not yelling at your kids, you are not spending enough time with them. You can also find Kristine at BLUNTmoms, Mock Mom or on the couch hogging the remote. Connect with her as @MumRevised on Facebook, Twitter, YouTube, Instagram and Pinterest.

Ashly Jeandel, Baby Bumping in France

Born in the heart of Canada, on the vast prairies in 1986, Ashly Jeandel grew up in the small town of Erickson, Manitoba. She lost her father when she was nineteen—to cancer and as she struggled to make sense of it all she filled her backpack and began a journey which would take her all over the world and finally to the small village of Ventron in Eastern France. There she met her husband and the adventure continued, with many challenges as she settled into a new culture. She is now married, has two children and runs her own successful business as an English consultant and teacher, clareellaconsulting.com. She and her husband also own a *gîte,* which enables Ashly to continue to meet new people from all over the world.

Jasmine Mah, Pride and (Bus) Prejudice

Jasmine grew up a second-generation Canadian in Edmonton, Alberta. A true romantic, she is an avid cook, wine drinker, and wanderluster. Jasmine studied Italian (and Russian, and Spanish and promptly forgot all but the former) and Pharmacy at the University of Alberta and thoroughly enjoyed her community pharmacy practice after graduating in 2013. She was a practicing pharmacist for just more than one year prior to packing her bags for Bergamo, Italy where she now resides indefinitely with her ridiculously good-looking Italian fiancé and an even handsomer cat, Puffo. She has written online for *Travel Fashion Girl, Pink Pangea,* and *Insiders Abroad* and was featured on an episode of

House Hunters International. She blogs about the search for the good life on questadolcevita.com (This Sweet Life) and is currently committed to writing in Italian for 365 days on The Jasmine & Jhumpa Project inspired by Pulitzer Prize author, Jhumpa Lahiri's "In Altre Parole". Also find her on Twitter and Instagram @questadolcevita.

Olga Mecking, Sun Worshipers

Olga Mecking is a writer and translator living in the Netherlands with her husband and three children. Olga writes about the expat life, travels and parenting on her blog, europeanmama.com. She has also been published on other websites, including the *Wall Street Journal, Scary Mommy, The Huffington Post* and *Babble.* When not blogging or thinking about blogging, Olga can be found reading, drinking tea and reading some more. Follow her blog and @The European Mama and on Facebook and Twitter.

Amanda van Mulligen, Losing My Grandmothers

Amanda van Mulligen is British, but has lived in the Netherlands since 2000, where she divides her time between writing, trying to Britify her Dutch children and getting to grips with the quirks of the locals. She is a contributing author to the expat anthology *Dutched Up! Rocking the Clogs Expat Style* and blogs about her expat way of living, loving and parenting: Expat Life with a Double Buggy lifewithadoublebuggy.blogspot.fr. You can find out more about Amanda van Mulligen and her writing on amandavanmulligen.com and Twitter: @AmandavMulligen.

Sarah Murdock, Mrs. Matt in West Africa

Sarah Murdock was glad to escape from eight years of working in Washington, DC to a life in rural Africa as a newlywed, where she lived as a missionary for fifteen years. She feels at home just about anywhere, having also grown up overseas, and dislikes being asked where she is from. She hopes to travel more with her family in the future, but for now is happily settled in Wyoming, USA with her husband and three children, enjoying the wild outdoors, seizing opportunities to pretend to be a cowgirl, and seeing moose from her bedroom window. She is a contributing author to *Knocked Up Abroad: Stories of pregnancy, birth and raising a family in a foreign country*, published in 2016 and available from Amazon both in print and e-book format.

Janneke Muyselaar-Jellema, *Choices*

Janneke Muyselaar-Jellema is a medical doctor. She has worked in the children and adolescent mental health field and in an asylum seekers' centre in the Netherlands, her passport country. Born and bred in Africa (Zambia, Malawi, Zimbabwe) she knows what it is like to grow up as a third culture kid. Her parents worked in Africa for over thirty-five years and she has travelled to more than twenty-five countries. Janneke loves reading and is passionate about raising kids in other cultures. She blogs at DrieCulturen.blogspot.fr. Janneke works in medical education and in a child rehabilitation centre. Twitter @DrieCulturen.

Akajiulonna Patricia Ndefo, *The Evolving Vocabulary of Expatriate Life*

Akajiulonna is a wife and mother of three adorable, keep-her-on-her-toes children. Embracing the expat trail she bid goodbye to Geosciences and her home country Nigeria and took up shop with her family in the Hague, Netherlands, Pau, France and now in Calgary, Canada. She had been featured on Hajel's Musings, discussing expat life, and her story in this book will be her first print publication. Patricia, as some of her friends fondly address her, enjoys reading, writing, soccer, board games and ladies hangouts. She also enjoys travelling and is learning the art of doing that successfully with her on-the-go trio. Akajiulonna is currently pursing a career in Human Resource Management.

Nitsa Olivadoti, Silent Competitions and Busted-Up Bus Stop Conversations

Nitsa Olivadoti is the author of *Cicada's Choice*, *Cicada's Consequence* and *Cicada's Closure* (due out end of 2016); a set of fictional novels based on her maternal grandmother's immigration experience. She graduated from Bridgewater State University in 2000 with a Fine Arts degree with a concentration in painting. Her visual work has been displayed in shows, online and local galleries and festivals. In recent years, she has moved her focus to writing abroad about her expat experiences. Nitsa chronicles her expat stories on Facebook as she continues to complete the Cicada Series and works on other fictional stories inspired by the countries she visits. You can find Cicada Series on Facebook and Twitter, Abroad-Short Story Blog on Facebook and you can also visit cicadaseries.com.

Margaret Ozemet, The Price of Beauty

Margaret Özemet is an American teacher and writer who fell madly in love and suddenly found herself sharing a tiny apartment with her new husband and his parents in Turkey. After a few years and a couple of kids, she's back in the US and trying to adapt. Her work has been seen on numerous online sites, print journals and anthologies, including *New Letters*, *Hippocampus*, *Red Fez Magazine* and *Scary Mommy* to name a few. Her work can also be seen on her weekly blog, Laughter is Better Than Prozac laughterisbetterthanprozac.wordpress.com. Keep up with her through her website: margaretozemet.com, on Twitter @MOzemet or on Facebook.

Lesley-Anne Price, Lost in Libya

Lesley-Anne is a mother of three children, Andrew, Kristina and Katherine. Born in Hong Kong, she lived there until she was ten years old and her family moved back to Scotland. She grew up in Helensburgh on the west coast of Scotland, initially studying History at Aberdeen University and ending with an honours degree in Sociology. After marrying her husband, Jonathan, in 1998, they moved to Pescara, Italy for one year. From Italy they moved to Libya, with their baby Andrew, where they lived for five years. Two daughters followed: Kristina, who was born in Libya and Katherine, who was born in Malta. The family returned to Aberdeen for three years, before their next posting to Kuala Lumpur, where they spent five years. Currently they are enjoying living in Houston.

Sally Rose, What Mattered Most

Born and raised in the piney woods of East Texas, Sally Rose lived in the Cajun Country of Louisiana, the plains of Oklahoma, the 'enchanted' land of New Mexico, and the Big Apple, New York City, before leaving the US for Santiago, Chile, where she now resides. Sally has been "telling tall tales from a long, skinny country" since 2009.

Sally's books include *Penny Possible*, the true story of a service dog in training, and *A Million Sticky Kisses*, the story of her first visits to Chile as a volunteer English teacher. She blogs on her website at iamsallyrose.com.

Amélie Sánchez, Riding the Subway

Amélie Sánchez was born and raised in France. In addition to her current expat assignment in Germany, she spent some of her childhood years in Iran and Tahiti and found it quite natural to move to the US upon marrying her American soul mate. She taught elementary school in Connecticut for seven years, a career she put on hold in order to explore her writing self in more depth while raising her two children.

Kathryn Streeter, One Trip Guaranteed to Stretch Your Marriage

Kathryn Streeter is a full-time writer, mother and wife. Highly mobile, she's moved twenty-two times in twenty-four years of marriage. Her writing has appeared in publications including *Literary Mama, Story|Houston, Scary Mommy, Elephant Journal, Mamalode, The Good Men Project, CSMonitor* and *Erma Bombeck. The Briar Cliff Review, Volume 26* published Streeter's essay "Through The Sand: A Driving Lesson From Dubai," a finalist in their Creative Nonfiction Contest. She is contributing author of best-selling anthology *Feisty After 45: The Best Blogs Of Midlife Women.* Find her at kathrynstreeter.com, on Instagram @kathrynstreeter and Twitter @streeterkathryn. Her essay in this book was originally published on *The Good Men Project.*

Kimberly Tremblay, The Dawn

Kimberly grew up in St. Albert, Canada where she obtained her B.Ed from the University of Alberta. After teaching for just over a year, she and her husband decided to move to Calgary, Canada where she continued to work as a teacher. Over time she became very interested in the mental well being of her students and completed a M.Ed in School Counselling. Kimberly then worked as a school counsellor for four years and had two children before moving to Kuala Lumpur, Malaysia. After a year she has settled into expat life and she shares her experience in this story, her first publication.

Catriona Turner, How Not to Say Goodbye

Catriona Turner started her writing life in Scotland with angsty adolescent poetry and music reviews for student newspapers. For ten years as an English teacher she moulded angsty adolescents into better writers. Now she's a parent and trailing spouse, and dabbling once again in her own wordsmithery. After spells in France and Uganda, she's now having a different francophone experience in the Republic of Congo. As The Frustrated Nester (thefrustratednester.com) she blogs about life in Africa, travel, and making each pitstop feel like home.

Lisa Webb, My (Naked) French Manicure and Stranded on a Non-Deserted Island

A seasoned expat, Lisa, her husband and their French-born children have called many places 'home'. Her family's love of travel has provided them with memories and experiences from across the globe, which she has used to author the bestselling children's book series, *The Kids Who Travel The World*. Lisa is a contributing author in numerous anthologies, using her expertise and passion to publish this book, *Once Upon an Expat*. You can find Lisa writing about life abroad and family travel on her blog Canadian Expat Mom (canadianexpatmom.com) and *The Huffington Post*.

Nicole Webb, Feels Like Home

Nicole was a news reader with 24-hour news channel, *Sky News Australia* for a decade, before stepping outside the box (literally) for a change of pace in Hong Kong with her hotelier husband and (then) bump. After a four-year love affair with the city that never sleeps, it was time to give up the skyscrapers and fragrant harbour and head north to the middle of China. Hello Xi'an! Almost two years into this hair-raising adventure, the trio have survived and thrived, learning enough Mandarin to order a coffee and stave off the many photographers, keen to capture the foreigners in all their glory! She's also collected enough fascinating and often unbelievable tales to tell a great story and is in the midst of writing her book on life in China. A passionate writer, Nicole has had her work published in magazines, online publications and media outlets across the globe.

Her biggest thrill is working on her critically acclaimed blog, Mint Mocha Musings: The Hotelier's Wife, an Expat Affair in Asia, mintmochamusings.com.

Chandi Wyant, Forbidden Falconing

As an independent woman from California, Chandi found the past three years in Qatar to be the most unusual of her international experiences. She has also been a solo expat in Italy, Switzerland and England. Italy is the place where Chandi's heart lies and has been since she first lived there at age twenty. Chandi's book about her forty-day pilgrimage walk in Italy will be published in 2017. When she's not dreaming in Italian, she is teaching history, writing about travel and expat life for her website, (paradiseofexiles.com), and sharing her photography on Instagram, @paradiseofexiles.

Gabrielle Yetter, A Year of Magic, Mystery and Chaos

Gabrielle Yetter is a writer who loves to travel... and a traveller who loves to write. She has lived in India, Bahrain, South Africa, England, the US and Mexico. She was a journalist in South Africa, owned a dining guide in San Diego, wrote a book about traditional Cambodian desserts and freelanced for publications and online sites in the US, the Netherlands, South Africa and Southeast Asia. In 2010, she and her husband, Skip, sold their home, quit their jobs, gave away most of their stuff and bought a one-way ticket to Cambodia. For the next three years, she volunteered with an NGO, wrote two books, *The Definitive Guide to Moving to Southeast Asia: Cambodia* and *The Sweet Tastes of Cambodia* and, in June 2015, co-authored *Just Go! Leave the Treadmill for a World of Adventure* with Skip. She and Skip are now house sitting around the world, taking care of homes and pets from Italy to Greece to Nicaragua. Visit her website GabrielleYetter.com and follow the couple's adventures on Facebook (The Meanderthals) and blog TheMeanderthals.com.

About Canadian Expat Mom

Lisa Webb is the creative mind behind Canadian Expat Mom, an expat/travel blog and boutique press. An English literature major and former educator, these days Lisa uses her time as an expat spouse to freelance write from across the globe. She penned Canadian Expat Mom's first publication, *The Kids Who Travel The World*, which launched as a bestselling children's book series. Now, Canadian Expat Mom is proud to publish its debut anthology, *Once Upon An Expat*, giving expat authors a platform to share their global stories.

You can read about Lisa's expat life and travels with her family at CanadianExpatMom.com.

If you've enjoyed reading the expat adventures in this book, please consider leaving a review on Amazon. Even one or two sentences can help future readers decide to purchase a copy of their own.

Printed in Poland
by Amazon Fulfillment
Poland Sp. z o.o., Wrocław